THE CHILDREN'S
The Adventures of Odys
By Padraic Colum
Illustrated by Willy Poga

This handsome reissue of the 1919 classic — with Willy Pogany's original line drawings — combines the immortal stories from Homer's *Iliad* and *Odyssey* into one glorious saga of heroism and magical adventure. Beloved by generations, Padraic Colum's masterful retelling of these epic adventures is remarkably fresh, consistently spellbinding and unmatched for its richness and poetry. It carries a new generation of young readers to ancient Greece with Odysseus and Achilles who, guided by the gods, seek vengeance against the Trojans, and follows Odysseus on his perilous journey — through the land of the Cyclopes, past Circe the Enchantress, the terrible Charybdis and the six-headed serpent Scylla.

The late Padraic Colum, poet, playwright, founder of the *Irish Review* and a leader of the Irish renaissance, is perhaps best known for his outstanding books for children. He was awarded the Regina Medal for his "distinguished contribution to children's literature," honoring works like *The Children of Odin, Roofs of Gold, The King of Ireland's Son, The Arabian Nights* and *The Golden Fleece* (*a* Newbery Honor Book).

THE
CHILDREN'S
HOMER

The Adventures of Odysseus and the Tale of Troy

by PADRAIC COLUM
illustrated by Willy Pogany

Macmillan/McGraw-Hill School Publishing Company
New York ▪ Chicago ▪ Columbus

Macmillan/McGraw-Hill School Division
10 Union Square East
New York, New York 10003

Printed in the United States of America

ISBN 0-02-179546-0 / 7, L.13A

4 5 6 7 8 9 WES 99 98 97 96 95 94

For HUGHIE and PETER this telling of
the world's greatest story because their
imaginations rise to deeds and wonders

CONTENTS

PART I

How Telemachus the son of Odysseus was moved to go
on a voyage in search of his father and how he heard from
Menelaus and Helen the tale of Troy

PART II

How Odysseus left Calypso's island and came to the land
of the Phaeacians; how he told he fared with the Cyclôpes
and went past terrible Scylla and Charybdis and came to
the island of Thrinacia where his men slaughtered the
cattle of the sun: how he was given a ship by the Phaeacians and came to his own land; how he overthrew the
wooers who wasted his substance and came to reign again
as king of Ithaka

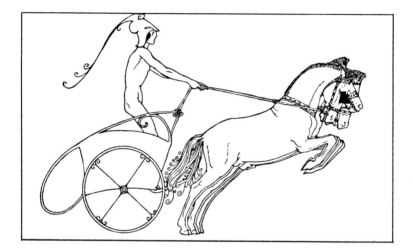

PART I

How Telemachus the son of Odysseus was moved to go on a voyage in search of his father and how he heard from Menelaus and Helen the tale of Troy

I

THIS is the story of Odysseus, the most renowned of all the heroes the Greek poets have told us of — of Odysseus, his wars and wanderings. And this story of Odysseus begins with his son, the youth who was called Telemachus.

It was when Telemachus was a child of a month old that a messenger came from Agamemnon, the Great King, bidding Odysseus betake himself to the war against Troy that the Kings and Princes of Greece were about to wage. The wise Odysseus, foreseeing the disasters that would befall all that entered that war, was loth to go. And so when Agamemnon's messenger came to the island of Ithaka where he was King, Odysseus pretended to be mad. And that the messenger, Palamedes, might believe he was mad indeed, he did a thing that no man ever saw being done before — he took an ass and an ox and yoked them together to the same plough and began to plough a field. And when he had ploughed a furrow he sowed it, not with seeds that would grow, but with salt. When Palamedes saw

him doing this he was nearly persuaded that Odysseus was mad. But to test him he took the child Telemachus and laid him down in the field in the way of the plough. Odysseus, when he came near to where the child lay, turned the plough aside and thereby showed that he was not a mad man. Then had he to take King Agamemnon's summons. And Agamemnon's word was that Odysseus should go to Aulis where the ships of the Kings and Princes of Greece were being gathered. But first he was to go into another country to seek the hero Achilles and persuade him also to enter the war against Troy.

And so Odysseus bade goodby to his infant son, Telemachus, and to his young wife, Penelope, and to his father, old Laertes. And he bade goodby to his house and his lands and to the island of Ithaka where he was King. He summoned a council of the chief men of Ithaka and commended to their care his wife and his child and all his household, and thereafter he took his sailors and his fighting men with him and he sailed away. The years went by and Odysseus did not return. After ten years the City was taken by the Kings and Princes of Greece and the thread of war was wound up. But still Odysseus did not return. And now minstrels came to Ithaka with word of the deaths or the homecomings of the heroes who had fought in the war against Troy. But no minstrel brought any word of Odysseus, of his death or of his appearance in any land known to men. Ten years more went by. And now that infant son whom he had left behind, Telemachus, had grown up and was a young man of strength and purpose.

II

ONE day, as he sat sad and disconsolate in the house of his father, the youth Telemachus saw a stranger come to the outer gate. There were many in the court outside, but no one went to receive the newcomer. Then, because he would never let a stranger stand at the gate without hurrying out to welcome him, and because, too, he had hopes that some day such a one would bring him tidings of his father, Telemachus rose up from where he was sitting and went down the hall and through the court and to the gate at which the stranger stood.

"Welcome to the house of Odysseus," said Telemachus giving him his hand. The stranger clasped it with a friendly clasp. "I thank you, Telemachus," he said, "for your welcome, and glad I am to enter the house of your father, the renowned Odysseus."

The stranger looked like one who would be a captain amongst soldiers. His eyes were gray and clear and shone wonderfully. In his hand he carried a great bronze spear. He and Telemachus went together through the court and into the hall. And when the stranger left his spear within the spearstand Telemachus took him to a high chair and put a footstool under his feet.

He had brought him to a place in the hall where the

crowd would not come. There were many in the court outside and Telemachus would not have his guest disturbed by questions or clamors. A handmaid brought water for the washing of his hands, and poured it over them from a golden ewer into a silver basin. A polished table was left at his side. Then the housedame brought wheaten bread and many dainties. Other servants set down dishes of meat with golden cups, and afterwards the maids came into the hall and filled up the cups with wine.

But the servants who waited on Telemachus and his guest were disturbed by the crowd of men who now came into the hall. They seated themselves at tables and shouted out their orders. Great dishes of meat were brought to them and bowls of wine, and the men ate and drank and talked loudly to each other and did not refrain even from staring at the stranger who sat with Telemachus.

"Is there a wedding-feast in the house?" the stranger asked, "or do the men of your clan meet here to drink with each other?"

A flush of shame came to the face of Telemachus. "There is no wedding-feast here," he said, "nor do the men of our clan meet here to drink with each other. Listen to me, my guest. Because you look so wise and because you seem so friendly to my father's name I will tell you who these men are and why they trouble this house."

Thereupon Telemachus told the stranger how his father had not returned from the war of Troy although it was now ten years since the City was taken by those with whom he went. "Alas," Telemachus said, "he must have died on his way back to us, and I must think that his bones lie under some nameless strait or channel of the ocean. Would he had died in the fight at Troy! Then the Kings and Princes would have made him a burial mound worthy of his name and his deeds. His memory would have been reverenced amongst men, and I, his son, would have a name, and would not be imposed upon by such men as you see here — men who are feasting and giving orders in my father's house and wasting the substance that he gathered."

"How come they to be here?" asked the stranger.

Telemachus told him about this also. When seven years had gone by from the fall of Troy and still Odysseus did not return there were those who thought he was dead and would never be seen more in the land of Ithaka. Then many of the young lords of the land wanted Penelope, Telemachus' mother, to marry one of them. They came to the house to woo her for marriage. But she, mourning for the absence of Odysseus and ever hoping that he would return, would give no answer to them. For three years now they were coming to the house of Odysseus to woo the wife whom he had left behind him. "They want to put my lady-mother between two dread difficulties," said Telemachus, "either to promise to wed one of them or to see the substance of our house wasted by them. Here they come and eat the bread of our fields, and slay the beasts of our flocks and herds, and drink the wine that in the old days my father laid up, and weary our servants with their orders."

When he had told him all this Telemachus raised his head and looked at the stranger: "O my guest," he said, "wisdom and power shine out of your eyes. Speak now to me and tell me what I should do to save the house of Odysseus from ruin. And tell me too if you think it possible that my father should still be in life."

The stranger looked at him with his gray, clear, wonderfully shining eyes. "Art thou verily the son of Odysseus?" said he.

"Verily, I am the son of Odysseus," said Telemachus.

"As I look at you," said the stranger, "I mark your head and eyes, and I know they are such a head and such eyes as Odysseus had. Well, being the son of such a man, and of such a woman as the lady Penelope, your spirit surely shall find a way of destroying those wooers who would destroy your house."

"Already," said Telemachus, "your gaze and your speech make me feel equal to the task of dealing with them."

"I think," said the stranger, "that Odysseus, your father, has not perished from the earth. He may yet win home through labors and perils. But you should seek for tidings of him. Harken to me now and I shall tell you what to do.

"Tomorrow summon a council of all the chief men of the land of Ithaka, and stand up in that council and declare that the time has come for the wooers who waste your substance to scatter, each man to his own home. And after the council has been held I would have you voyage to find out tidings of your father, whether he still lives and where he might be. Go to Pylos first, to the home of Nestor, that old King who was with your father in the war of Troy. Beg Nestor to give you whatever tidings he has of Odysseus. And from Pylos go to Sparta, to the home of Menelaus and Helen, and beg tidings of your father from them too. And if you get news of his being alive, return: It will be easy for you then to endure for another year the wasting of your substance by those wooers. But if you learn that your father, the renowned Odysseus, is indeed dead and gone, then come back, and in your own country raise a great funeral mound to his memory, and over it pay all funeral rites. Then let your mother choose a good man to be her husband and let her marry him, knowing for a certainty that Odysseus will never come back to his own house. After that something will remain for you to do: You will have to punish those wooers who destroy the goods your father gathered and who insult his house by their presence. And when all these things have been done, you, Telemachus, will be free to seek out your own fortune: you will rise to fame, for I mark that you are handsome and strong and most likely to be a wise and valiant man. But now I must fare on my journey."

The stranger rose up from where he sat and went with Telemachus from the hall and through the court and to the outer gate. Telemachus said: "What you have told me I shall not forget. I know you have spoken out of a wise and a friendly heart, and as a father to his son."

The stranger clasped his hands and went through the gate. And then, as he looked after him Telemachus saw the stranger change in his form. He became first as a woman, tall, with fair hair and a spear of bronze in her hand. And then the form of a woman changed too. It changed into a great sea-eagle that on wide wings rose up and flew high through the air. Telemachus knew then that his visitor was an immortal and no other than the goddess Athene who had been his father's friend.

III

WHEN Telemachus went back to the hall those who were feasting there had put the wine cups from them and were calling out for Phemius, the minstrel, to come and sing some tale to delight them. And as he went amongst them one of the wooers said to another, "The guest who was with him has told Telemachus something that has changed his bearing. Never before did I see him hold himself so proudly. Mayhap he has spoken to him of the return of his father, the renowned Odysseus."

Phemius came and the wooers called upon him to sing them a tale. And the minstrel, in flowing verse, began the tale of the return of the Kings and Princes from Troy, and of how some god or goddess put a trouble upon them as they left the City they had taken. And as the minstrel began the tale, Penelope, Telemachus' lady-mother, was coming down the stairs with two handmaids beside her.

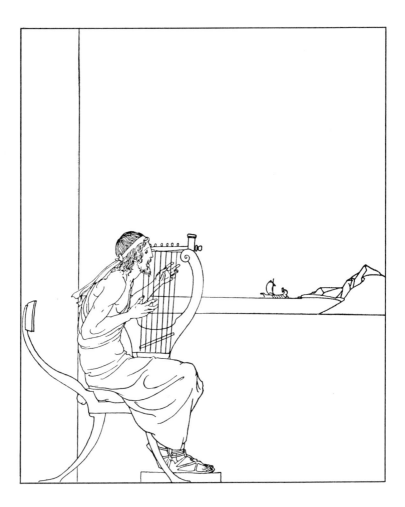

She heard the words he sang, and she stood still in her grief and drew her veil across her face. "O Phemius," she cried, "cease from that story that ever wastes my heart — the story that has brought me sorrow and that leaves me comfortless all my days! O Phemius, do you not know other tales of men and gods that you might sing in this hall for the delight of my noble wooers?"

The minstrel would have ceased when Penelope spoke thus to him, but Telemachus went to the stairway where his lady-mother stood, and addressed her.

"My lady-mother," said he, "why should you not let the minstrel delight the company with such songs as the spirit moves him to give us? It is no blame to him if he sings of that which is sorrowful to us. As for you, my mother, you must learn to endure that story, for long will it be sung and far and wide. And you are not the only one who is bereaved — many another man besides Odysseus lost the happy days of his homecoming in the war of Troy."

Penelope, his lady-mother, looked in surprise at the youth who spoke to her so wisely. Was this indeed Telemachus who before had hardly lifted his head? And as she looked at him again she saw that he carried his head — that head of his that was so like Odysseus' — high and proudly. She saw that her son was now indeed a man. Penelope spoke no word to him, for a new thought had come into her mind. She turned round on the stairs and went back with her handmaids to the chamber where her loom and her distaff were. And as she went up the stairway and away from them her wooers muttered one to the other that she would soon have to choose one of them for her husband.

Telemachus turned to those who were standing at the tables and addressed them. "Wooers of my mother," he said, "I have a word to say to you."

"By the gods, youth," said one of the wooers, "you must tell us first who he is who has made you so high and proud of speech."

"Surely," said another, "he who has done that is the stranger who was with him. Who is he? Why did he come here, and of what land has he declared himself to be?"

"Why did he not stay so that we might look at him and speak to him?" said another of the wooers.

"These are the words I would say to you. Let us feast now in peace, without any brawling amongst us, and listen to the tale that the minstrel sings to us," said Telemachus. "But tomorrow let us have a council made up of the chief men of this land of Ithaka. I shall go to the council and speak there. I shall ask that you leave this house of mine and feast on goods that you yourselves have gathered. Let the chief men judge whether I speak in fairness to you or not. If you do not heed what I will say openly at the council, before all the chief men of our land, then let it be on your own heads what will befall you."

All the wooers marvelled that Telemachus spoke so boldly. And one said, "Because his father, Odysseus, was King, this youth thinks he should be King by inheritance. But may Zeus, the god, never grant that he be King."

Then said Telemachus, "If the god Zeus should grant

that I be King, I am ready to take up the Kingship of the land of Ithaka with all its toils and all its dangers." And when Telemachus said that he looked like a young king indeed.

But they sat in peace and listened to what the minstrel sang. And when evening came the wooers left the hall and went each to his own house. Telemachus rose and went to his chamber. Before him there went an ancient woman who had nursed him as a child — Eurycleia was her name. She carried burning torches to light his way. And when they were in his chamber Telemachus took off his soft doublet and put it in Eurycleia's hands, and she smoothed it out and hung it on the pin at his bedside. Then she went out and she closed the door behind with its handle of silver and she pulled the thong that bolted the door on the other side. And all night long Telemachus lay wrapped in his fleece of wool and thought on what he would say at the council next day, and on the goddess Athene and what she had put into his heart to do, and on the journey that was before him to Nestor in Pylos and to Menelaus and Helen in Sparta.

IV

AS soon as it was dawn Telemachus rose from his bed. He put on his raiment, bound his sandals on his feet, hung his sharp sword across his

shoulder, and took in his hand a spear of bronze. Then he went forth to where the Council was being held in the open air, and two swift hounds went beside him.

The chief men of the land of Ithaka had been gathered already for the council. When it was plain that all were there, the man who was oldest amongst them, the lord Ægyptus, rose up and spoke. He had sons, and two of them were with him yet, tending his fields. But one, Eurynomous by name, kept company with the wooers of Telemachus' mother. And Ægyptus had had another son; he had gone in Odysseus' ship to the war of Troy, and Ægyptus knew he had perished on his way back. He constantly mourned for his son, and thinking upon him as he spoke, Ægyptus had tears in his eyes.

"Never since Odysseus summoned us together before he took ship for the war of Troy have we met in council," said he. "Why have we been brought together now? Has someone heard tidings of the return of Odysseus? If it be so, may the god Zeus give luck to him who tells us of such good fortune."

Telemachus was glad because of the kindly speech of the old man. He rose up to speak and the herald put a staff into his hands as a sign that he was to be listened to with reverence. Telemachus then spoke, addressing the old lord Ægyptus.

"I will tell you who it is," he said, "who has called the men of Ithaka together in council, and for what purpose. Revered lord Ægyptus, I have called you together, but not because I have had tidings of the return of my father, the renowned Odysseus, nor because I would speak to you about some affair of our country. No. I would speak to you all because I suffer and because I am at a loss — I, whose father was King over you, praised by you all. Odysseus is long away from Ithaka, and I deem that he will never return. You have lost your King. But you can put another King to rule over you. I have lost my father, and I can have no other father in all my days. And that is not all my loss, as I will show you now, men of Ithaka.

"For three years now my mother has been beset by men who come to woo her to be wife for one of them. Day after day they come to our house and kill and devour our beasts and waste the wine that was laid up against my father's return. They waste our goods and our wealth. If I were nearer manhood I would defend my house against them. But as yet I am not able to do it, and so I have to stand by and see our house and substance being destroyed."

So Telemachus spoke, and when his speech was ended Antinous, who was one of the wooers, rose up.

"Telemachus," said he, "why do you try to put us to shame in this way? I tell all here that it is not we but your mother who is to blame. We, knowing her husband Odysseus is no longer in life, have asked her to become the wife of one of us. She gives us no honest answer. Instead she has given her mind to a device to keep us still waiting.

"I will tell you of the council what this device is. The lady Penelope set up a great loom in her house and began to weave a wide web of cloth. To each of us she sent a message saying that when the web she was working at was woven, she would choose a husband from amongst us. 'Laertes, the father of Odysseus, is alone with one to care for him living or dead,' said she to us. 'I must weave a shroud for him against the time which cannot now be far off when old Laertes dies. Trouble me not while I do this. For if he should die and there be no winding-sheet to wrap him round all the women of the land would blame me greatly.'

"We were not oppressive and we left the lady Penelope to weave the web, and the months have gone by and still the web is not woven. But even now we have heard from one of her maids how Penelope tries to finish her task. What she weaves in the daytime she unravels at night. Never, then, can the web be finished and so does she try to cheat us.

"She has gained praise from the people for doing this. 'How wise is Penelope,' they say, 'with her devices.' Let her be satisfied with their praise then, and leave us alone. We too have our devices. We will live at her house and eat and drink there and give orders to her servants and we shall see which will satisfy her best — to give an answer or to let the wealth of her house be wasted.

"As for you, Telemachus, I have these words to say to you. Lead your mother from your father's house and to the house of her father, Icarius. Tell Icarius to give her in marriage to the one she chooses from amongst us. Do this and no more goods will be wasted in the house that will be yours."

Then Telemachus rose and said, "Never will I lead my

mother out of a house that my father brought her into. Quit my father's house, or, as I tell you now, the day may come when a doom will fall upon you there for your insolence in it."

And even as Telemachus spoke, two eagles from a mountain crest flew over the place where the council was being held. They wheeled above and flapped their wings and looked down upon the crowd with destruction in their gaze. They tore each other with their talons, and then flew away across the City.

An old man who was there, Halitherses by name, a man skilled in the signs made by birds, told those who were around what was foreshown by the combat of the eagles in the air. "Odysseus," he said, "is not far from his friends. He will return, and his return will mean affliction for those who insult his house. Now let them make an end of their mischief." But the wooers only laughed at the old man, telling him he should go home and prophesy to his children.

Then arose another old man whose name was Mentor, and he was one who had been a friend and companion of Odysseus. He spoke to the council saying:

"Never again need a King be gentle in his heart. For kind and gentle to you all was your King, Odysseus. And now his son asks you for help and you do not hurry to give it him. It is not so much an affliction to me that these wooers waste his goods as that you do not rise up to forbid it. But let them persist in doing it on the hazard of their own heads. For a doom will come on them, I say. And I say again to you of the council: you are many and the wooers are few: Why then do you not put them away from the house of Odysseus?"

But no one in the council took the side of Telemachus and Halitherses and Mentor — so powerful were the wooers and so fearful of them were the men of the council. The wooers looked at Telemachus and his friends with mockery. Then for the last time Telemachus rose up and spoke to the council.

"I have spoken in the council, and the men of Ithaka know, and the gods know, the rights and wrongs of my case. All I ask of you now is that you give me a swift ship with twenty youths to be my crew so that I may go to Pylos and to Sparta to seek tidings of my father. If I find he is alive and that he is returning, then I can endure to wait another year in the house and submit to what you do there."

Even at this speech they mocked. Said one of them, Leocritus by name, "Though Odysseus be alive and should one day come into his own hall, that would not affright us. He is one, and we are many, and if he should strive with those who outnumber him, why then, let his doom be on his own head. And now, men of the council, scatter yourselves and go each to his own home, and let Mentor and Halitherses help Telemachus to get a ship and a crew."

Leocritus said that knowing that Mentor and Halitherses were old and had few friends, and that they could do nothing to help Telemachus to get a ship. The council broke up and those who were in it scattered. But the wooers went together back to the house of Odysseus.

V

TELEMACHUS went apart, and, going by himself, came to the shore of the sea. He dipped his hands into the seawater and prayed, saying, "O Goddess Athene, you who did come to my father's hall yesterday, I have tried to do as you bade me. But still the wooers of my mother hinder me from taking ship to seek tidings of my father."

He spoke in prayer and then he saw one who had the likeness of the old man Mentor coming toward him. But by the gray, clear, wonderfully shining eyes he knew that the figure was none other than the goddess Athene.

"Telemachus," said she, "if you have indeed one drop of your father's blood in you or one portion of his spirit, if you are as he was — one ready to fulfil both word and work, your voyage shall not be in vain. If you are different from what he was, I have no hope that you will accomplish your desire. But I have seen in you something of the wisdom and the courage of Odysseus. Hear my counsel then, and do as I direct you. Go back to your father's house and be with the wooers for a time. And get together corn and barley-flour and wine in jars. And while you are doing all this I will gather together a crew for your ship.

There are many ships in sea-girt Ithaka and I shall choose the best for you and we will rig her quickly and launch her on the wide deep."

When Telemachus heard her counsel he tarried no more but went back to the house and stood amongst the wooers, and when he had spoken with them he went down into the treasure-vault. It was a spacious room filled with gold and bronze and chests of raiment and casks of wine. The doors of that vault were closed night and day and Eurycleia, the dame who had been the nurse of Telemachus when he was little, guarded the place. She came to him, and he spoke to her:

"My nurse," said he, "none but yourself must know what I would do now, and you must swear not to speak of it to my lady-mother until twelve days from this. Fill twelve jars with wine for me now, and pour twelve measures of barley-meal into well-sewn skins. Leave them all together for me, and when my mother goes into the upper chamber, I shall have them carried away. Lo, nurse, I go to Pylos and to Sparta to seek tidings from Nestor and Menelaus of Odysseus, my father."

When she heard him say this, the nurse Eurycleia lamented. "Ah, wherefore, dear child," she cried, "has such a thought risen in your mind? How could you fare over wide seas and through strange lands, you who were never from your home? Stay here where you are well beloved. As for your father, he has long since perished amongst strangers — why should you put yourself in danger to find out that he is no more? Nay, do not go, Telemachus, my fosterling, but stay in your own house and in your own well-beloved country."

Telemachus said: "Dear nurse, it has been shown to me that I should go by a goddess. Is not that enough for you and for me? Now make all ready for me as I have asked you, and swear to me that you will say nothing of it to my mother until twelve days from this, or until she shall miss me herself."

Having sworn as he asked her, the nurse Eurycleia drew the wine into jars and put the barley-meal into the well-sewn skins. Telemachus left the vault and went back again into the hall. He sat with the wooers and listened to the minstrel Phemius sing about the going forth of Odysseus to the wars of Troy.

And while these things were happening the goddess Athene went through the town in the likeness of Telemachus. She went to this youth and that youth and told them of the voyage and asked them to make ready and go down to the beach where the boat would be. And then she went to a man called Noëmon, and begged him for a swift ship, and Noëmon gave it her.

When the sun sank and when the ways were darkened Athene dragged the ship to where it should be launched and brought the tackling to it. The youths whom Athene had summoned — they were all of the age of Telemachus — came, and Athene aroused them with talk of the voyage. And when the ship was ready she went to the house of Odysseus. Upon the wooers who were still in the hall she caused sleep to fall. They laid their heads upon the

tables and slumbered beside the wine cups. But Athene sent a whisper through the hall and Telemachus heard and he rose up and came to where she stood. Now she had on the likeness of old Mentor, the friend of his father Odysseus.

"Come," said she, "your friends are already at the oars. We must not delay them."

But some of the youths had come with the one whom they thought was old Mentor. They carried with Telemachus the skins of corn and the casks of wine. They came to the ship, and Telemachus with a cheer climbed into it. Then the youths loosed the ropes and sat down at the benches to pull the oars. And Athene, in the likeness of old Mentor, sat at the helm.

And now they set up the mast of pine and they made it fast with forestays, and they hauled up the sails with ropes of twisted oxhide. And a wind came and filled out the sails, and the youths pulled at the oars, and the ship dashed away. All night long Telemachus and his friends sat at the oars and under the sails, and felt the ship bearing them swiftly onward through the dark water. Phemius, the minstrel, was with them, and, as the night went by, he sang to them of Troy and of the heroes who had waged war against it.

VI

TROY, the minstrel sang, was the greatest of the Cities of men; it had been built when the demigods walked the earth; its walls were so strong and so high that enemies could not break nor scale them; Troy had high towers and great gates; in its citadels there were strong men well armed, and in its treasuries there were stores of gold and silver. And the King of Troy was Priam. He was old now, but he had sons that were good Captains. The chief of them all was Hector.

Hector, the minstrel sang, was a match for any warrior the nations could send against Troy. Because he was noble and generous as well as brave, the people were devoted to him. And Hector, Priam's son, was commander in the City.

But Priam had another son who was not counted amongst the Captains. Paris was his name. Now when Paris was in his infancy, a soothsayer told King Priam that he would bring trouble upon Troy. Then King Priam had the child sent away from the City. Paris was reared amongst country people, and when he was a youth he herded sheep.

Then the minstrel sang of Peleus, the King of Phthia, and of his marriage to the river nymph, Thetis. All the gods and goddesses came to their wedding feast. Only one of the immortals was not invited — Eris, who is Discord. She came, however. At the games that followed the wedding feast she threw a golden apple amongst the guests, and on the apple was written "For the fairest."

Each of the three goddesses who was there wished to be known as the fairest and each claimed the golden apple — Aphrodite who inspired love; Athene who gave wisdom; and Hera who was the wife of Zeus, the greatest of the gods. But no one at the wedding would judge between the goddesses and say which was the fairest. And then the shepherd Paris came by, and him the guests asked to give judgment.

Said Hera to Paris, "Award the apple to me and I will give you a great kingship." Said Athene, "Award the golden apple to me and I will make you the wisest of men." And Aphrodite came to him and whispered, "Paris, dear Paris, let me be called the fairest and I will make you beautiful, and the fairest woman in the world will be your wife." Paris looked on Aphrodite and in his eyes she was the fairest. To her he gave the golden apple and ever afterwards she was his friend. But Hera and Athene departed from the company in wrath.

The minstrel sang how Paris went back to his father's City and was made a prince of Troy. Through the favor of Aphrodite he was the most beautiful of youths. Then Paris went out of the City again. Sent by his father he went to Tyre. And coming back to Troy from Tyre he went through Greece.

Now the fairest woman in the world was in Greece; she was Helen, and she was married to King Menelaus. Paris saw her and loved her for her beauty. And Aphrodite inspired Helen to fall in love with Paris. He stole her from the house of Menelaus and brought her into Troy.

King Menelaus sent to Troy and demanded that his wife be given back to him. But the people of Troy, thinking no King in the world could shake them, and wanting to boast that the fairest woman in the world was in their city, were not willing that Menelaus be given back his wife. Priam and his son, Hector, knew that a wrong had been done, and knew that Helen and all that she had brought with her should be given back. But in the council there were vain men who went against the word of Priam and Hector, declaring that for no little King of Greece would they give up Helen, the fairest woman in all the world.

Then the minstrel sang of Agamemnon. He was King of rich Mycenæ, and his name was so high and his deeds were so renowned that all the Kings of Greece looked to him. Now Agamemnon, seeing Menelaus, his brother, flouted by the Trojans, vowed to injure Troy. And he spoke to the Kings and Princes of Greece, saying that if they all united their strength they would be able to take the great city of Troy and avenge the slight put upon Menelaus and win great glory and riches for themselves.

And when they had come together and had taken note of their strength, the Kings and Princes of Greece thought well of the word of Agamemnon and were eager to make war upon Troy. They bound themselves by a vow to take the City. Then Agamemnon sent messages to the heroes whose lands were far away, to Odysseus, and to Achilles, who was the son of Peleus and Thetis, bidding them also enter the war.

In two years the ships of all the Kings and Princes were gathered into Aulis and the Greeks, with their leaders, Agamemnon, Aias, Diomedes, Nestor, Idomeneus, Achilles and Odysseus, sailed for the coast of Troy. One hero after another subdued the cities and nations that were the allies of the Trojans, but Troy they did not take. And the minstrel sang to Telemachus and his fellow-voyagers how year after year went by, and how the host of Greeks still remained between their ships and the walls of the City, and how in the ninth year there came a plague that smote with death more men than the Trojans killed.

So the ship went on through the dark water, very swiftly, with the goddess Athene, in the likeness of old Mentor, guiding it, and with the youths listening to the song that Phemius the minstrel sang.

VII

THE sun rose and Telemachus and his fellow-voyagers drew near to the shore of Pylos and to the steep citadel built by Neleus, the father of Nestor, the famous King. They saw on the shore men in companies making sacrifice to Poseidon, the dark-haired god of the sea. There were nine companies there and each company had nine black oxen for the sacrifice, and the number of men in each company was five hundred. They slew the oxen and they laid parts to burn on the altars of the god, and the men sat down to feast.

The voyagers brought their ship to the shore and Telemachus sprang from it. But before him went the goddess, gray-eyed Athene, in the likeness of the old man, Mentor. And the goddess told Telemachus that Nestor, the King whom he had come to seek, was on the shore. She bade him now go forward with a good heart and ask Nestor for tidings of his father, Odysseus.

But Telemachus said to her, "Mentor, how can I bring myself to speak to one who is so reverenced? How should I greet him? And how can I, a young man, question such a one as Nestor, the old King?"

The goddess, gray-eyed Athene, encouraged him; the right words, she said, would come. So Telemachus went forward with his divine companion. Nestor was seated on the shore with his sons around him. And when they saw the two strangers approach, the sons of Nestor rose up to greet them. One, Peisistratus, took the hand of Telemachus and the hand of the goddess and led them both to where Nestor was.

A golden cup was put into the hand of each and wine was poured into the cups, and Nestor's son, Peisistratus, asked Telemachus and the goddess to pray that the sacri-

fice they were making to Poseidon, the god of the sea, would bring good to them and to their people. Then the goddess Athene in the likeness of old Mentor held the cup in her hand and prayed:

"Hear me, Poseidon, shaker of the earth: First to Nestor and his sons grant renown. Then grant to the people of Pylos recompense for the sacrifice of oxen they have made. Grant, too, that Telemachus and I may return safely when what we have come in our our swift ship to seek has been won."

Telemachus prayed in the words of the goddess and then the sons of Nestor made them both sit on the fleeces that were spread on the shore. And dishes of meat were brought to them and cups of wine, and when they had eaten and drunk, the old King, Nestor, spoke to them.

"Until they have partaken of food and drink, it is not courteous," he said, "to ask of strangers who they are and whither they go. But now, my guests, I will ask of you what your land is, and what your quest, and what names you bear."

Then Telemachus said: "Nestor, renowned King, glory of the Greeks, we have come out of Ithaka and we seek tidings of my father, of Odysseus, who, long ago, fought by your side in the war of Troy. With you, men say, he sacked the great City of the Trojans. But no further story about him has been told. And I have come to your knees, O King, to beg you to give me tidings of him — whether he died and you saw his death, or whether you heard of his death from another. And if you should answer me, speak not, I pray you, in pity for me, but tell me all you know or have heard. Ah, if ever my father helped you in the land of the Trojans, by the memory of what help he gave, I pray you speak in truth to me, his son."

Then said Nestor, the old King, "Verily, my son, you bring sorrow to my mind. Ah, where are they who were with me in our war against the mighty City of Troy? Where is Aias and Achilles and Patroklos and my own dear son, Antilochos, who was so noble and so strong? And where is Agamemnon now? He returned to his own land, to be killed in his own hall by a most treacherous foeman. And now you ask me of Odysseus, the man who was dearer to me than any of the others — Odysseus, who was always of the one mind with me! Never did we two speak diversely in the assembly nor in the council.

"You say to me that you are the son of Odysseus! Surely you are. Amazement comes over me as I look on you and listen to you, for you look as he looked and you speak as he spoke. But I would have you speak further to me and tell me of your homeland and of how things fare in Ithaka."

Then he told the old King of the evil deeds worked by the wooers of his mother, and when he had told of them Telemachus cried out, "Oh, that the gods would give me such strength that I might take vengeance on them for their many transgressions."

Then said old Nestor, "Who knows but Odysseus will win home and requite the violence of these suitors and the insults they have offered to your house. The goddess Athene might bring this to pass. Well was she inclined to your father, and never did the gods show such favor to a mortal as the gray-eyed goddess showed to Odysseus, your father."

But Telemachus answered, "In no wise can your word be accomplished, King."

Then Athene, in the likeness of old Mentor, spoke to him and said, "What word has crossed your lips, Telemachus? If it should please them, any one of the gods could bring a man home from afar. Only this the gods may not do — avert death from a man who has been doomed to it."

Telemachus answered her and said, "Mentor, no longer let us talk of these things. Nestor, the renowned King, has been very gracious to me, but he has nothing to tell me of my father. I deem now that Odysseus will never return."

"Go to Menelaus," said Nestor. "Go to Menelaus in Sparta. Lately he has come from a far and a strange country and it may be that he has heard of Odysseus in his wanderings. You can go to Sparta in your ship. But if you have a mind to fare by land then will I give you a chariot and horses, and my son will go with you to be a guide for you into Sparta."

Then Telemachus, with Athene, the gray-eyed goddess in the likeness of old Mentor, would have gone back to their ship, but Nestor the King said, "Zeus forbid that you two should go back to the ship to take your rest while there is guest-room in my hall. Come with me to a place where you can lie softly. Never shall it be said that a son of Odysseus, my dear friend, lay on the hard deck of a ship while I am alive and while children of mine are left in my hall. Come with me now."

Then the goddess Athene in the likeness of old Mentor said, "You have spoken as becomes you, renowned King. Telemachus should harken to your word and go with you. But it is meet that the young men who came for the love of him should have an elder with them on the ship tonight. I shall abide with them."

So speaking, the goddess, gray-eyed Athene, in the likeness of old Mentor went from the shore, and Telemachus went with Nestor and his sons to the high citadel of Neleus. And there he was given a bath, and the maiden Polycaste, the youngest daughter of King Nestor, attended him. She gave him new raiment to wear, a goodly mantle and doublet. He slept in a room with Peisistratus, the youngest of Nestor's sons.

In the morning they feasted and did sacrifice, and when he had given judgments to the people, the old King Nestor spoke to his sons:

"Lo, now, my sons. Yoke for Telemachus the horses to the chariot that he may go on his way to Sparta."

The sons of Nestor gave heed and they yoked the swift horses to the chariot and the housedame came from the hall and placed within the chariot wine and dainties. Telemachus went into the chariot and Peisistratus sat before him. Then Peisistratus touched the horses with the whip and they sprang forward, and the chariot went swiftly over the plain. Soon they left behind them the steep citadel of Neleus and the land of Pylos. And when the sun sank and the ways were darkened, they came to Pheræ and to the house of Diocles and there they rested for the night.

In the morning as soon as the sun rose they yoked the horses and they mounted the chariot, and for another day they journeyed across the plain. They had gone far and the ways were again darkened around them.

VIII

THEY came to Sparta, to a country lying low amongst the hills, and they stayed the chariot outside the gate of the King's dwelling. Now upon that day Menelaus was sending his daughter into Phthia, with horses and chariots, as a bride for Achilles' son. And for Megapenthes, his own son, a bride was being brought into the house. Because of these two marriages there was feasting in the palace and kinsmen and neighbors were gathered there. A minstrel was singing to the guests and two tumblers were whirling round the high hall to divert them.

To the King in his high hall came Eteoneus, the steward. "Renowned Menelaus," said Eteoneus, "there are two strangers outside, men with the looks of heroes. What would you have me do with them? Shall I have their horses unyoked, bidding them enter the Palace, or shall I let them fare on to another dwelling?"

"Why do you ask such a question, Eteoneus?" said Menelaus in anger. "Have we not eaten the bread of other men on our wanderings, and have we not rested ourselves in other men's houses? Knowing this you have no right to ask whether you should bid strangers enter or let them go past the gate of my dwelling. Go now and bid them enter and feast with us."

Then Eteoneus went from the hall, and while he had servants unyoke the horses from their chariot he led Telemachus and Peisistratus into the palace. First they were brought to the bath, and when they had come from the bath refreshed, they were given new cloaks and mantles. When they had dressed themselves they were led into the King's high hall. They seated themselves there, and a maid brought water in a golden ewer and poured it over their hands into a silver basin. Then a polished table was put beside them, and the housedame placed bread and meat and wine upon it so that they might eat.

Menelaus came to where they sat and said to Telemachus and Peisistratus, "By your looks I know you to be of the line of Kings. Eat now, and when you have refreshed yourselves I will ask who you are and from what place you come."

But before they had finished their meal, and while yet Menelaus the king was showing them the treasures that were near, the lady Helen came into the high hall — Helen for whom the Kings and Princes of Greece had gone to war. Her maids were with her, and they set a chair for her near where Menelaus was and they put a rug of soft wool under her feet. Then one brought to her a silver basket filled with colored yarn. And Helen sat in her high chair and took the distaff in her hands and worked the yarn.

She questioned Menelaus about the things that had happened during the day, and as she did she watched Telemachus.

Then the lady Helen left the distaff down and said, "Menelaus, I am minded to tell you who one of these strangers is. No one was ever more like another than this youth is like great-hearted Odysseus. I know that he is no other than Telemachus, whom Odysseus left as a child, when, for my sake, the Greeks began their war against Troy."

Then said Menelaus, "I too mark his likeness to Odysseus. The shape of his head, the glance of his eye, remind me of Odysseus. But can it indeed be that Telemachus has come into my house?"

"Renowned Menelaus," said Peisistratus, "this is indeed the son of Odysseus. And I avow myself to be the son of another comrade of yours, of Nestor, who was with you at the war of Troy. I have been sent with Telemachus to be his guide to your house."

Menelaus rose up and clasped the hand of Telemachus. "Never did there come to my house," said he, "a youth more welcome. For my sake did Odysseus endure much toil and many adventures. Had he come to my country I would have given him a city to rule over, and I think that nothing would have parted us, one from the other. But Odysseus, I know, has not returned to his own land of Ithaka."

Then Telemachus, thinking upon his father, dead, or wandering through the world, wept. Helen, too, shed tears, remembering things that had happened. And Menelaus, thinking upon Odysseus and on all his toils, was silent and sad; and sad and silent too was Peisistratus, thinking upon Antilochos, his brother, who had perished in the war of Troy.

But Helen, wishing to turn their minds to other thoughts, cast into the wine a drug that lulled pain and brought forgetfulness — a drug which had been given to her in Egypt by Polydamna, the wife of King Theon. And when they had drunk the wine their sorrowful memories went from them, and they spoke to each other without regretfulness. Thereafter King Menelaus told of his adventure with the Ancient One of the Sea — the adventure that had brought to him the last tidings of Odysseus.

IX

SAID Menelaus, "Over against the river that flows out of Egypt there is an Island that men call Pharos, and to that island I came with my ships when we, the heroes who had fought at Troy, were separated one from the other. There I was held, day after day, by the will of the gods. Our provision of corn was spent and my men were in danger of perishing of hunger. Then one day while my companions were striving desperately to get fish out of the sea, I met on the shore one who had pity for our plight.

"She was an immortal, Eidothëe, a daughter of the

Ancient One of the Sea. I craved of her to tell me how we might get away from that place, and she counselled me to take by an ambush her father, the Ancient One of the Sea, who is also called Proteus. 'You can make him tell you,' said she, 'for he knows all things, what you must do to get away from this island of Pharos. Moreover, he can declare to you what happened to the heroes you have been separated from, and what has taken place in your own hall.'

"Then said I to that kind nymph Eidothëe, 'Show me how I may take by an ambush your immortal father, the Ancient One of the Sea.'

"Said Eidothëe, 'My father, Proteus, comes out of the sea when the sun is highest in the heavens. Then would he lie down to sleep in the caves that are along the shore. But before he goes to sleep he counts, as a shepherd counts his flock, the seals that come up out of the ocean and lie round where he lies. If there be one too many, or one less than there should be, he will not go to sleep in the cave. But I will show you how you and certain of your companions may be near without the Ancient One of the Sea being aware of your presence. Take three of your men — the three you trust above all the others — and as soon as it is dawn tomorrow meet me by the edge of the sea.'

"So saying the nymph Eidothëe plunged into the sea and I went from that place anxious, but with hope in my heart.

"Now as soon as the dawn had come I walked by the seashore and with me came the three that I trusted above all my companions. The daughter of the Ancient One of the Sea, Eidothëe, came to us. In her arms she had the skins of seals newly slain, one for each of us. And at the cave where the seals lay she scooped holes in the sand and bade us lie there, covering ourselves with the skins. Then she spoke to me and said:

" 'When my father, the Ancient One of the Sea, comes here to sleep, lay hands upon him and hold him with all the strength you have. He will change himself into many shapes, but do not you let go your hold upon him. When he changes back into the shape he had at first you may let go your holds. Question him then as to how you may leave this place, or question him as to any other matter that may be on your mind, and he will answer you, speaking the truth.'

"We lay down in the holes she had scooped in the sand and she covered each of us with one of the skins she had brought. Then the seals came out of the sea and lay all around us. The smell that came from those beasts of the sea afflicted us, and it was then that our adventure became terrible. We could not have endured it if Eidothëe had not helped us in this also. She took ambrosia and set it beneath each man's nostril, so that what came to us was not the smell of the sea-beasts but a divine savor. Then the nymph went back to the sea.

"We lay there with steadfast hearts amongst the herd of seals until the sun was at its highest in the heavens. The Ancient One of the Sea came out of the ocean depths. He went amongst the seals and counted them, and us four men he reckoned amongst his herd. Then in great contentment he laid himself down to sleep.

"We rushed upon him with a cry and laid hold on him with all the strength of our hands. But we had no sooner grasped him than his shape changed. He became a lion and faced us. Yet we did not let go of our grasp. He became a serpent, yet we still held him. He became a leopard and then a mighty boar; he became a stream of water and then a flowering tree. Yet still we held to him with all our might and our hearts were not daunted by the shapes he changed to before our eyes. Then, seeing that he could not make us loose our hold, the Ancient One of the Sea, who was called Proteus, ceased in his changes and became as we had seen him first.

" 'Son of Atreus,' said he, speaking to me, 'who was it showed you how to lay this ambush for me?'

" 'It is for you who know all things,' said I, 'to make answer to us. Tell me now why it is that I am held on this island? Which of the gods holds me here and for what reason?'

"Then the Ancient One of the Sea answered me, speaking truth, 'Zeus, the greatest of all the gods holds you here. You neglected to make sacrifice to the gods and for that reason you are held on this island.'

" 'Then,' said I, 'what must I do to win back the favor of the gods?'

"He told me, speaking truth, 'Before setting sail for your own land,' he said, 'you must return to the river Ægyptus that flows out of Africa, and offer sacrifice there to the gods.'

"When he said this my spirit was broken with grief. A

long and a grievous way would I have to sail to make that sacrifice, turning back from my own land. Yet the will of the gods would have to be done. Again I was moved to question the Ancient One of the Sea, and to ask him for tidings of the men who were my companions in the wars of Troy.

"Ah, son of Odysseus, more broken than ever was my spirit with grief when he told me of their fates. Then I heard how my brother, great Agamemnon, reached his own land and was glad in his heart. But his wife had hatred for him, and in his own hall she and Ægisthus had him slain. I sat and wept on the sands, but still I questioned the Ancient One of the Sea. And he told me of strong Aias and how he was killed by the falling rock after he had boasted that Poseidon, the god of the Sea, could afflict him no more. And of your father, the renowned Odysseus, the Ancient One had a tale to tell.

"Then, and even now it may be, Odysseus was on an island away from all mankind. 'There he abides in the hall of the nymph Calypso,' the Ancient One of the Sea told me. 'I saw him shed great tears because he could not go from that place. But he has no ship and no companions and the nymph Calypso holds him there. And always he longs to return to his own country, to the land of Ithaka.' And after he had spoken to me of Odysseus, he went from us and plunged into the sea.

"Thereafter I went back to the river Ægyptus and moored my ships and made pious sacrifice to the gods. A fair wind came to us and we set out for our own country.

Swiftly we came to it, and now you see me the happiest of all those who set out to wage war against Troy. And now, dear son of Odysseus, you know what an immortal told of your father — how he is still in life, but how he is held from returning to his own home."

Thus from Menelaus the youth Telemachus got tiding of his father. When the King ceased to speak they went from the hall with torches in their hands and came to the vestibule where Helen's handmaids had prepared beds for Telemachus and Peisistratus. And as he lay there under purple blankets and soft coverlets, the son of Odysseus thought upon his father, still in life, but held in that unknown island by the nymph Calypso.

X

HIS ship and his fellow-voyagers waited at Pylos, but for a while longer Telemachus bided in Sparta, for he would fain hear from Menelaus and from Helen the tale of Troy. Many days he stayed, and on the first day Menelaus told him of Achilles, the greatest of the heroes who had fought against Troy, and on another day the lady Helen told him of Hector, the noblest of all the men who defended King Priam's City.

"Achilles," said King Menelaus, "was sprung of a race that was favored by the immortals. Peleus, the father of Achilles, had for his friend, Cheiron, the wisest of the

Centaurs — of those immortals who are half men and half horse. Cheiron it was who gave to Peleus his great spear. And when Peleus desired to wed an immortal, Zeus, the greatest of the gods, prevailed upon the nymph Thetis to marry him, although marriage with a mortal was against her will. To the wedding of Thetis and Peleus all the gods came. And for wedding gifts Zeus gave such armor as no mortal had ever worn before — armor wonderfully bright and wonderfully strong, and he gave also two immortal horses.

"Achilles was the child of Thetis and Peleus — of an immortal woman married to a mortal hero. He grew up most strong and fleet of foot. When he was grown to be a youth he was sent to Cheiron, and his father's best friend instructed him in all the ways of war. He became the greatest of spearmen, and on the mountain with the Centaur he gained in strength and in fleetness of foot.

"Now after he returned to his father's hall the war against Troy began to be prepared for. Agamemnon, the king, wanted Achilles to join the host. But Thetis, knowing that great disasters would befall those who went to that war, feared for Achilles. She resolved to hide him so that no word from King Agamemnon might reach him. And how did the nymph Thetis hide her son? She sent him to King Lycomedes and prayed the King to hide Achilles amongst his daughters.

"So the youth Achilles was dressed as a maiden and stayed with the daughters of the King. The messengers of Agamemnon searched everywhere for him. Many of them

came to the court of King Lycomedes, but not finding one like Achilles amongst the King's sons they went away.

"Odysseus, by Agamemnon's order, came to seek Achilles. He knew that the youth was not amongst the King's sons. He saw the King's daughters in their father's orchard, but could not tell if Achilles was amongst them, for all were veiled and dressed alike.

"Then Odysseus went away and returned as a peddler carrying in his pack such things as maidens admire — veils and ornaments and brazen mirrors. But under the veils and ornaments and mirrors the wise Odysseus left a gleaming sword. When he came before the maidens in the King's orchard he laid down his peddler's pack. The mirrors and veils and ornaments were taken up and examined eagerly. But one of the company took up the gleaming sword and looked at it with flashing eyes. Odysseus knew that this was Achilles, King Peleus' son.

"He gave the youth the summons of King Agamemnon, bidding him join the war that the Kings and Princes of Greece were about to wage against Troy. And Achilles was glad to get the summons and glad to go. He returned to Phthia, to his father's citadel. There did he make ready to go to Aulis where the ships were being gathered. He took with him his father's famous warriors, the Myrmidons who were never beaten in battle. And his father bestowed on him the armor and the horses that had been the gift of Zeus — the two immortal horses Xanthos and Balios.

"But what rejoiced Achilles more than the gift of marvellous armor and immortal steeds was that his dear comrade, Patroklos, was to be with him as his mate in war. Patroklos had come into Phthia and into the hall of Peleus when he was a young boy. In his own country he had killed another boy by mischance over a game of dice. His father, to save him from the penalty, fled with him to King Peleus. And Achilles' father gave them refuge and took Patroklos into his house and reared him up with his own son. Later he made him squire to Achilles. These two grew up together and more than brothers they loved each other.

"Achilles bade goodby to Phthia, and to his hero-father and his immortal mother, and he and Patroklos with the Myrmidons went over the sea to Aulis and joined the host of the Kings and Princes who had made a vow not to refrain from war until they had taken King Priam's famous city."

XI

ACHILLES became the most renowned of all the heroes who strove against Troy in the years the fighting went on. Before the sight of him, clad in the flashing armor that was the gift of Zeus and standing in the chariot drawn by the immortal horses, the Trojan ranks would break and the Trojan men would flee back to the gate of their city. And many lesser cities and towns around Troy did the host with the help of Achilles take.

"Now because of two maidens taken captive from some of these cities a quarrel between Achilles and Agamemnon grew up. One of the maidens was called Chryseis and the other Briseis. Chryseis was given to Agamemnon and Briseis to Achilles.

"The father of Chryseis was a priest of Apollo, and when the maiden, his daughter, was not given back to him, he went and prayed the god to avenge him on the host. Apollo listened to his prayer, and straightway the god left his mountain peak with his bow of silver in his hands. He stood behind the ships and shot his arrows into the host. Terrible was the clanging of his silver bow. He smote the beasts of the camp first, the dogs and the mules and the horses, and then he smote the men, and those whom his arrows smote were stricken by the plague.

"The warriors began to die, and every day more perished by the plague than were killed by the spears and swords and arrows of the Trojans. Now a council was summoned and the chiefs debated what was to be done to save the host. At the council there was a soothsayer named Kalchas; he stood up and declared that he knew the cause of the plague, and he knew too how the remainder of the host might be saved from it.

"It was because of the anger of Apollo, Kalchas said; and that anger could only be averted by Agamemnon sending back to his father, the priest of Apollo, the maiden Chryseis.

"Then was Agamemnon wroth exceedingly. 'Thou seer of things evil,' said he to Kalchas, 'never didst thou see aught of good for me or mine. The maiden given to me, Chryseis, I greatly prize. Yet rather than my folk should perish I shall let her be taken from me. But this let you all of the council know: some other prize must be given to me that the whole host may know that Agamemnon is not slighted.'

"Then said Achilles: 'Agamemnon, of all Kings you are the most covetous. The best of us toil and battle that you may come and take what part of the spoil may please you. Be covetous no more. Let this maiden go back to her father and afterwards we will give you some other prize.'

"Said Agamemnon: 'The council here must bind itself to give me recompense.'

" 'Still you speak of recompense, Agamemnon,' answered Achilles. 'No one gains more than you gain. I had no quarrel with the men of Troy, and yet I have come here, and my hands bear the brunt of the war.'

" 'You who are captains must give me a recompense,' said Agamemnon, 'or else I shall go to the tent of Achilles and take away the maiden given to him, Briseis of the Fair Cheeks.'

" 'I am wearied of making war for you,' answered Achilles. 'Though I am always in the strife but little of the spoil comes to my tent. Now will I depart to my own land, to Phthia, for I am not minded to stay here and be dishonored by you, O King.'

" 'Go,' said Agamemnon, 'if your soul be set upon fleeing, go. But do not think that there are not captains and heroes here who can make war without you. Go and lord it amongst your Myrmidons. Never shall we seek your aid. And that all may know I am greater than you, Achilles, I shall go to your tent and take away the maiden Briseis.'

"When he heard Agamemnon's speech the heart within Achilles' breast was divided, and he knew not whether he should remain still and silent in his anger, or, thrusting the council aside, go up to Agamemnon and slay him with the sword. His hand was upon the sword-hilt when an immortal appeared to him — the goddess Athene. No one in the company but Achilles was aware of her presence. 'Draw not the sword upon Agamemnon,' she said, 'for equally dear to the gods are you both.' Then Achilles drew back and thrust his heavy sword into its sheath again. But although he held his hand he did not refrain from angry and bitter words. He threw down on the ground the staff that had been put into his hands as a sign that he was to be listened to in the council. 'By this staff that no more shall bear leaf or blossom,' he said, 'I swear that longing for Achilles' aid shall come upon the host of Agamemnon, but that no Achilles shall come to their help. I swear that I shall let Hector triumph over you.'

"Then the council broke up and Achilles with Patroklos, his dear comrade, went back to their tent. A ship was launched and the maiden Chryseis was put aboard and Odysseus was placed in command. The ship set out for Chryse. There on the beach they found the priest of

Apollo, and Odysseus placed his daughter in the old man's arms. They made sacrifice to Apollo, and thereafter the plague was averted from the host.

"But to Achilles' tent there came the messengers of the King, and they took Briseis of the Fair Cheeks and led her away. Achilles, in bitter anger, sat by the sea, hard in his resolve not to help Agamemnon's men, no matter what defeat great Hector inflicted upon them."

XII

SUCH was the quarrel, dear son, between Agamemnon, King of men, and great Achilles. Ah, because of that quarrel many brave men and great captains whom I remember went down to their deaths!

"But Agamemnon before long relented and he sent three envoys to make friendship between himself and Achilles. The envoys were Odysseus and Aias and the old man Phoinix who had been a fosterfather to Achilles. Now when these three went into his hut they found Achilles sitting with a lyre in his hands, singing to the music he made. His song was of what Thetis, his goddess-mother, had told him concerning his own fate — how, if he remained in the war against Troy, he should win for himself imperishable renown but would soon lose his life, and how, if he left the war, his years in his own land should be long, although no great renown would be his. Patroklos, his dear friend, listened to what Achilles sang. And Achilles sang of what royal state would be his if he gave up the war against the Trojans and went back to his father's halls — old Peleus would welcome him, and he would seek a bride for him from amongst the loveliest of the Greek maidens. 'In three days,' he sang, 'can Poseidon, God of the Sea, bring me to my own land and to my father's royal castle.'

" 'Well dost thou sing, Achilles,' said Odysseus to him, 'and pleasant would it be to hear thy song if our hearts were not filled up with great griefs. But have not nine years passed away since we came here to make war on Troy? And now are not our ships' timbers rotted and their tacklings loosed, and do not many of our warriors think in their hearts how their wives and children have long been waiting for their return? And still the walls of Troy rise up before us as high and as unconquerable as ever! No wonder our hearts are filled up with griefs. And now Achilles, the greatest of our heroes, and the Myrmidons, the best of our warriors, have left us and gone out of the fight.'

" 'Even today did great Hector turn back our battalions that were led by Agamemnon and Aias and Diomedes, driving us to the wall that we have built around our ships. Behind that wall we halted and called one to the other to find out who had escaped and who had fallen in the onslaught Hector made. Only when he had driven us behind our wall did Hector turn back his chariot and draw off his men.

" 'But Hector has not gone through the gates of the City. Look now, Achilles! His chariots remain on the plain. Lo now, his watchfires! A thousand fires thou canst see and beside each sits fifty warriors with their horses loose beside their chariots champing barley. Eagerly they wait for the light of the dawn when they will come against us again, hoping this time to overthrow the wall we have builded, and come to our ships and burn them with fire, and so destroy all hope of our return.'

" 'We are all stricken with grief and fear. Even Agamemnon weeps. We have seen him standing before us like unto a dark fountain breaking from some beetling cliff. How else could he but weep tears? Tomorrow it may be he shall have to bid the host draw the ships to the water and depart from the coast of Troy. Then will his name forever be dishonored because of defeat and the loss of so many warriors.'

" 'Deem'st thou I grieve for Agamemnon's griefs, Odysseus?' said Achilles. 'But although thou dost speak of Agamemnon thou art welcome, thou and thy companions. Even in my wrath you three are dear to me.'

"He brought them within the hut and bade a feast be prepared for them. To Odysseus, Aias, and Phoinix wine cups were handed. And when they had feasted and drunk wine, Odysseus turned to where Achilles sat on his bench in the light of the fire, and said:

" 'Know, Achilles, that we three are here as envoys from King Agamemnon. He would make a friendship with thee again. He has injured and he has offended thee, but all that a man can do he will do to make amends. The maiden

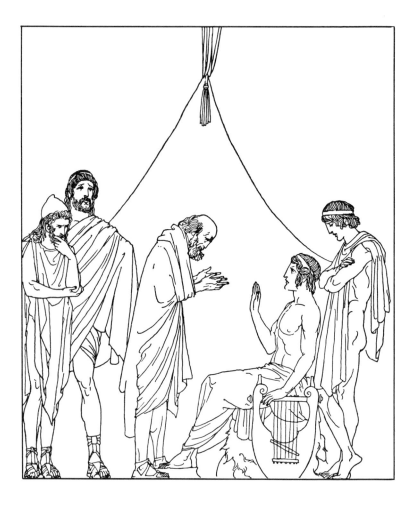

Briseis he will let go back. Many gifts will he give thee too, Achilles. He will give thee seven tripods, and twenty cauldrons, and ten talents of gold. Yes, and besides, twelve royal horses, each one of which has triumphed in some race. He who possesses these horses will never lack for wealth as long as prizes are to be won by swiftness. And harken to what more Agamemnon bade us say to thee. If we win Troy he will let thee load your ship with spoil of the city — with gold and bronze and precious stuffs. And thereafter, if we win to our homes he will treat thee as his own royal son and will give thee seven cities to rule over. And if thou wilt wed there are three daughters in his hall — three of the fairest maidens of the Greeks — and the one thou wilt choose he will give thee for thy wife, Chryso-themis, or Laodike, or Iphianassa.'

"So Odysseus spoke and then Aias said, 'Think, Achil-les, and abandon now thy wrath. If Agamemnon be hate-ful to thee and if thou despiseth his gifts, think upon thy friends and thy companions and have pity upon them. Even for our sakes, Achilles, arise now and go into battle and stay the onslaught of the terrible Hector.'

"Achilles did not answer. His lion's eyes were fixed upon those who had spoken and his look did not change at all for all that was said.

"Then the old man Phoinix who had nurtured him went over to him. He could not speak, for tears had burst from him. But at last, holding Achilles' hands, he said:

" 'In thy father's house did I not rear thee to greatness — even thee, most noble Achilles. With me and with none other wouldst thou go into the feasthall, and, as a child, thou would'st stay at my knee and eat the morsel I gave, and drink from the cup that I put to thy lips. I reared thee, and I suffered and toiled much that thou mightst have strength and skill and quickness. Be thou merciful in thy heart, Achilles. Be not wrathful any more. Cast aside thine anger now and save the host. Come now. The gifts Agamemnon would give thee are very great, and no king nor prince could despise them. But if without gifts thou would'st enter the battle, then above all heroes the host would honor thee.'

"Achilles answered Phoinix gently and said, 'The honor the host would bestow upon me I have no need of, for I am honored in the judgment of Zeus, the greatest of the gods, and while breath remains with me that honor cannot pass away. But do thou, Phoinix, stay with me, and many things I shall bestow upon thee, even the half of my kingdom. Ah, but urge me not to help Agamemnon, for if thou dost I shall look upon thee as a friend to Agamemnon, and I shall hate thee, my fosterfather, as I hate him.'

"Then to Odysseus, Achilles spoke and said, "Son of Laertes, wisest of men, harken now to what I shall say to thee. Here I should have stayed and won that imperishable renown that my goddess-mother told me of, even at the cost of my young life if Agamemnon had not aroused the wrath that now possesses me. Know that my soul is implacable toward him. How often did I watch out sleepless nights, how often did I spend my days in bloody battle for the sake of Agamemnon's and his brother's cause! Why are we here if not because of lovely Helen? And yet one whom I cherished as Menelaus cherished Helen has been taken from me by order of this King! He would let her go her way now! But no, I do not desire to see Briseis ever again, for everything that comes from Agamemnon's hand is hateful to me. Hateful are all the gifts he would bestow upon me, and him and his treasures I hold at a straw's worth. I have chosen. Tomorrow I shall have my Myrmidons draw my ships out to the sea, and I shall depart from Troy for my own land.'

"Said Aias, 'Have the gods, Achilles, put into your breast a spirit implacable and proud above all men's spirits?'

" 'Yes, Aias,' said Achilles. 'My spirit cannot contain my wrath. Agamemnon has treated me, not as a leader of armies who won many battles for him, but as a vile sojourner in his camp. Go now and declare my will to him. Never again shall I take thought of his war.'

"So he spoke, and each man took up a two-handled cup and poured out wine as an offering to the gods. Then Odysseus and Aias in sadness left the hut. But Phoinix remained, and for him Patroklos, the dear friend of Achilles, spread a couch of fleeces and rugs.

"Odysseus and Aias went along the shore of the sea and by the line of the ships and they came to where Agamemnon was with the greatest of the warriors of the host. Odysseus told them that by no means would Achilles join in the battle, and they all were made silent with grief. Then Diomedes, the great horseman, rose up and said, 'Let

Achilles stay or go, fight or not fight, as it pleases him. But it is for us who have made a vow to take Priam's city, to fight on. Let us take food and rest now, and tomorrow let us go against Hector's host, and you, Agamemnon, take the foremost place in the battle.'

"So Diomedes spoke and the warriors applauded what he said, and they all poured out libations of wine to the gods, and thereafter they went to their huts and slept. But for Agamemnon, the King, there was no sleep that night. Before his eyes was the blaze of Hector's thousand watch-fires and in his ears were the sound of pipes and flutes that made war-music for the Trojan host encamped upon the plain."

XIII

WHEN dawn came the King arrayed himself for the battle, putting on his great breastplate and his helmet that had a high plume of horse-hair; fastening about his legs greaves fitted with ankle-clasps of silver; and hanging round his shoulders a great sword that shone with studs of gold — a sword that had a silver scabbard fitted with golden chains. Over his shoulders he cast a great lion's skin, and he took upon his arm a shield that covered the whole of a man. Next he took in his hands two strong spears of bronze, and so arrayed and so armed he was ready to take the foremost place in the battle.

"He cried aloud and bade the Greeks arm themselves, and straightway they did so and poured from behind the wall that guarded their ships into the Trojan plain. Then the chiefs mounted their chariots, and their charioteers turned the horses toward the place of battle.

"Now on the high ground before them the Trojans had gathered in their battalions and the figure of great Hector was plain to Agamemnon and his men. Like a star that now and then was hidden by a cloud, so he appeared as he went through the battalions, all covered with shining bronze. Spears and arrows fell upon both sides. Footmen kept slaying footmen and horsemen kept slaying horsemen with the sword, and the dust of the plain rose up, stirred by the thundering hooves of the horses. From dawn till morning and from morning till noon the battle raged, but at midday the Greeks broke through the Trojan lines. Then Agamemnon in his chariot rushed through a gap in the line. Two men did he instantly slay, and dashing onward he slew two warriors who were sons of King Priam. Like fire falling upon a wood and burning up the underwood went King Agamemnon through the Trojan ranks, and when he passed many strong-necked horses rattled empty chariots, leaving on the earth the slain warriors that had been in them. And through the press of men and up to the high walls of Troy did Agamemnon go, slaying Trojan warriors with his spear. Hector did not go nigh him, for the gods had warned Hector not to lead any onslaught until Agamemnon had turned back from battle.

"But a Trojan warrior smote King Agamemnon on the midarm, below the elbow, and the point of his spear went

clean through. Still he went through the ranks of the Trojans, slaying with spear and sword. And then the blood dried upon his wound and a sharp pain came upon him and he cried out, 'O friends and captains! It is not possible for me to war forever against the Trojans, but do you fight on to keep the battle from our ships.' His charioteer turned his horses, and they, all covered with foam and grimed with dust, dashed back across the plain bearing the wounded King from that day's battle.

"Then Hector sprang to the onslaught. Leaping into his chariot he led the Trojans on. Nine captains of the Greeks he slew in the first onset. Now their ranks would have been broken, and the Greeks would have fled back to their ships if Odysseus had not been on that wing of the battle with Diomedes, the great horseman. Odysseus cried out, 'Come hither, Diomedes, or verily Hector will sweep us across the plain and bring the battle down to our ships.'

"Then these two forced themselves through the press of battle and held back the onset of Hector till the Greeks had their chance to rally. Hector spied them and swept in his chariot toward them. Diomedes lifted his great spear and flung it full at Hector. The bronze of the spear struck the bronze of his helmet, and bronze by bronze was turned. The blow told upon Hector. But he, springing from his chariot, stayed amongst the press of warriors, resting himself on his hands and knees. Darkness was before his eyes for a while, but he got breath again, and leaping back into his chariot drove away from that dangerous place.

"Then Diomedes himself received a bitterer wound, for Paris, sheltering himself behind a pillar on the plain, let fly an arrow at him. It went clean through his **right** foot. Odysseus put his shield before his friend and comrade, and Diomedes was able to draw the arrow from his flesh. But Diomedes was fain to get back into his chariot and to command his charioteer to drive from the battle.

"Now Odysseus was the only one of the captains who stayed on that side of the battle, and the ranks of the Trojans came on and hemmed him round. One warrior struck at the center of his shield and through the shield the strong Trojan spear passed and wounded the flesh of Odysseus. He slew the warrior who had wounded him and he drew the spear from his flesh, but he had to give ground. But loudly as any man ever cried, Odysseus cried out to the other captains. And strong Aias heard him and drew near, bearing his famous shield that was like a tower. The Trojan warriors that were round him drew back at the coming of Aias, and Odysseus went from the press of battle, and mounting his chariot drove away.

"Where Aias fought the Trojans gave way, and on that side of the battle they were being driven back toward the City. But suddenly upon Aias there fell an unaccountable dread. He cast behind him his great shield, and he stood in a maze, like a wild bull, turning this way and that, and slowly retreating before those who pressed toward him. But now and again his valor would come back and he would stand steadily and, with his great shield, hold at bay the Trojans who were pressing toward the ships.

Arrows fell thick upon his shield, confusing his mind. And Aias might have perished beneath the arrows if his comrades had not drawn him to where they stood with shields sloping for a shelter, and so saved him.

"All this time Hector was fighting on the left wing of the battle against the Greeks, who were led by Nestor and Idomeneus. And on this side Paris let fly an arrow that brought trouble to the enemies of his father's City. He struck Machaon who was the most skilled healer of wounds in the whole of the host. And those who were around Machaon were fearful that the Trojans would seize the stricken man and bear him away. Then said Idomeneus, 'Nestor, arise. Get Machaon into your chariot and drive swiftly from the press of battle. A healer such as he is worth the lives of many men. Save him alive so that we may still have him to draw the arrows from our flesh and put medicaments into our wounds.' Then did Nestor lift the healer into his chariot, and the charioteer turned the horses and they too drove from the press of battle and toward the hollow ships."

XIV

ACHILLES, standing by the stern of his great ship, saw the battle as it went this way and that way, but his heart was not at all moved with pity for the destruction wrought upon the Greeks. He saw the chariot of Nestor go dashing by, dragged by sweating horses, and he knew that a wounded man was in the chariot. When it had passed he spoke to his dear friend Patroklos.

" 'Go now, Patroklos,' he said, 'and ask of Nestor who it is that he has borne away from the battle.'

" 'I go, Achilles,' Patroklos said, and even as he spoke he started to run along the line of the ships and to the hut of Nestor.

"He stood before the door, and when old Nestor beheld him he bade him enter. 'Achilles sent me to you, revered Nestor,' said Patroklos, 'to ask who it was you bore out of the battle wounded. But I need not ask, for I see that it is none other than Machaon, the best of our healers.'

" 'Why should Achilles concern himself with those who are wounded in the fight with Hector?' said old Nestor. 'He does not care at all what evils befall the Greeks. But thou, Patroklos, wilt be grieved to know that Diomedes and Odysseus have been wounded, and that sore-wounded is Machaon whom thou seest here. Ah, but Achilles will have cause to lament when the host perishes beside our burning ships and when Hector triumphs over all the Greeks.'

"Then the old man rose up and taking Patroklos by the hand led him within the hut, and brought him to a bench beside which lay Machaon, the wounded man.

" 'Patroklos,' said Nester, 'speak thou to Achilles. Nay, but thy father bade thee spake words of counsel to thy friend. Did he not say to thee 'turn Achilles from harsh courses by gentle words'? Remember now the words of thy father, Patroklos, and if ever thou did'st speak to Achilles with gentle wisdom speak to him now. Who knows but thy words might stir up his spirit to take part in the battle we have to fight with Hector?'

" 'Nay, nay, old man,' said Patroklos, 'I may not speak to Achilles to ask for such a thing.'

" 'Then,' said Nestor, 'do thou thyself enter the war and bring Achilles' Myrmidons with thee. Then might we who are wearied with fighting take breath. And beg of Achilles to give you his armor that you may wear it in the battle. If thou would'st appear clad in Achilles' bronze the Trojans would think that he had entered the war again and they would not force the fight upon us.'

"What old Nestor said seemed good to Patroklos and he left the hut and went back along the ships. And on his way he met Eurypylos, a sorely wounded man, dragging himself from the battle, and Patroklos helped him back to his hut and cheered him with discourse and laid healing herbs upon his wounds.

"And even as he left old Nestor's hut, Hector was before the wall the Greeks had builded to guard their ships. On came the Trojans against that wall, holding their shields of bulls' hides before them. From the towers that were along the wall the Greeks flung great stones upon the attackers.

"Over the host an eagle flew, holding in its talons a blood-red serpent. The serpent struggled with the eagle and the eagle with the serpent, and both had sorely wounded each other. But as they flew over the host of the Greeks and Trojans the serpent struck at the eagle with his fangs, and the eagle, wounded in the breast, dropped the serpent. Then were the Trojans in dread, seeing the blood-red serpent across their path, for they thought it was an omen from Zeus. They would have turned back from the wall in fear for this omen had not Hector pressed them on. 'One omen is best, I know,' he cried, 'to fight a good fight for our country. Forward then and bring the battle to those ships that came to our coast against the will of the gods.'

"So Hector spoke. Then he lifted up a stone — such a stone as not two of the best of men now living could as much as raise from the ground — and he flung this stone full at the strongly set gate. It broke the hinges and the bars, and the great gate fell under the weight of the tremendous stone. Then Hector leaped across it with two spears in his hands. No warrior could withstand him now And as the Trojans scaled the walls and poured across the broken gate, the Greeks fled to their ships in terror and dismay.

"Patroklos saw the gate go down and the Trojans pour toward the ships in a mass that was like a great rock rolling down a cliff. Idomeneus and Aias led the Greeks who fought to hold them back. Hector cast a spear at Aias and struck him where the belt of his shield and the belt of his sword crossed. Aias was not wounded by the stroke. Then Aias cast at Hector a great stone that was used to prop a ship. He struck him on the breast, just over the rim of his shield. Under the weight of that blow great Hector spun round like a top. The spear fell from his hands and the

bronze of his shield and helmet rang as he fell on the ground.

"Then the Greeks dashed up to where Hector lay, hoping to drag him amongst them. But his comrades placed their shields around him and drove back the warriors that were pressing round. They lifted Hector into his chariot, and his charioteer drove him from the place of battle groaning heavily from the hurt of that terrible blow.

"Now the Greeks rallied and came on with a shout, driving the Trojans back before them. The swift horses under Hector's chariot brought him out on the plain. They who were with him lifted him out, and Hector lay gasping for breath and with black blood gushing from him. And then as he lay there stricken he heard the voice of a god — even of Apollo — saying, 'Hector, son of Priam, why dost thou lie fainting, apart from the host? Dost thou not know that the battle is desperate? Take up thy spirit again. Bid thy charioteer drive thee toward the ships of the Greeks.'

"Then Hector rose and went amongst the ranks of his men and roused up their spirits and led them back to the wall. And when the Greeks saw Hector in fighting trim again, going up and down the ranks of his men, they were affrighted.

"He mounted his chariot and he shouted to the others, and the Trojan charioteers lashed their horses and they came on like a great wave. They crossed the broken wall again and came near the ships. Then many of the Greeks got into their ships and struck at those who came near with long pikes.

"And all around the ships companies of Greek warriors stood like rocks that the sea breaks against in vain. Nestor cried out to the Greeks, bidding them fight like heroes, or else lose in the burning ships all hope of return to their native land. Aias, a long pike in his hand, drove multitudes of Trojans back, while, in a loud voice, he put courage into the Greeks. Hector fought his way forward crying to the Trojans to bring fire to the ships that had come to their coast against the will of the gods.

"He came to the first of the ships and laid his hand upon its stern. Many fought against him there. Swords and spears and armor fell on the ground, some from the hands, some off the shoulders of warring men, and the black earth was red with blood. But Hector was not driven away from the ship. And he shouted 'Bring fire that we may burn the ships that have brought the enemy to our land. The woes we have suffered were because of the cowardice of the elders of the City — they would not let me bring my warriors here and bring battle down to the ships when first they came to our beach. Do not let us return to the City until we have burned the ships with fire.'

"But whoever brought fire near the ship was stricken by strong Aias who stood there with a long pike in his hands. Now all this time Patroklos sat in the hut of Eurypylos, the wounded man he had succoured, cheering him with discourse and laying healing herbs on his wounds.

But when he saw fire being brought to the ships he rose up and said, 'Eurypylos, no longer may I stay here although great is your need of attendance. I must get aid for our warriors.' Straightway he ran from the hut and came to where Achilles was.

" 'If thy heart, Achilles,' he said, 'is still hard against the Greeks, and if thou wilt not come to their aid, let me go into the fight and let me take with me thy company of Myrmidons. And O Achilles, grant me another thing. Let me wear thine armor and thy helmet so that the Trojans will believe for a while that Achilles has come back into the battle. Then would they flee before me and our warriors would be given a breathing-time.'

"Said Achilles, 'I have declared that I shall not cease from my wrath until the Trojans come to my own ships. But thou, Patroklos, dear friend, may'st go into the battle. All thou hast asked shall be freely given to thee — my Myrmidons to lead and my armor to wear, and even my chariot and my immortal horses. Drive the Trojans from the ships. But when thou hast driven them from the ships, return to this hut. Do not go near the City. Return, I bid thee, Patroklos, when the Trojans are no longer around the ships, and leave it to others to battle on the plain.'

"Then Patroklos put on the armor that Zeus had given to Achilles' father, Peleus. Round his shoulders he cast the sword of bronze with its studs of silver, and upon his head he put the helmet with its high horse-hair crest — the terrible helmet of Achilles. Then Achilles bade the charioteer yoke the horses to the chariot — the horses,

Xanthos and Balios, that were also gifts from the gods. And while all this was being done Achilles went amongst the Myrmidons, making them ready for the battle and bidding them remember all the threats they had uttered against the Trojans in the time when they had been kept from the fight.

"Then he went back to his hut and opening the chest that his mother, Thetis, had given him he took from it a four-handled cup — a cup that no one drank out of but Achilles himself. Then pouring wine into this cup and holding it toward Heaven, Achilles prayed to Zeus, the greatest of the gods:

'My comrade I send to the war, O far-seeing Zeus:
May'st strengthen his heart, O Zeus, that all triumph be
    his:
But when from the ships he hath driven the spear of our
    foes,
Out of the turmoil of battle may he to me return
Scathless, with arms and his comrades who fight hand to
    hand.'

"So Achilles prayed, and the Myrmidons beside their ships shouted in their eagerness to join in the battle."

XV

WHO was the first of the great Trojan Champions to go down before the onset of Patroklos? The first was Sarpedon who had come with an army to help Hector from a City beyond Troy. He saw the Myrmidons fight round the ships and break the ranks of the Trojans and quench the fire on the half-burnt ship. He saw that the warrior who had the appearance of Achilles affrighted the Trojans so that they turned their horses' heads toward the City. The Myrmidons swept on with Patroklos at their head. Now when he saw him rushing down from the ships Sarpedon threw a dart at Patroklos. The dart did not strike him. Then Patroklos flung a spear and struck Sarpedon even at the heart. He fell dead from his chariot and there began a battle for his body — the Trojans would have carried it into the City, so that they might bury with all honor the man who had helped them, and the Greeks would have carried it away, so that, having his body and his armor, the slaying of Sarpedon might be more of a triumph for them.

"So a battle for his body went on. Now Sarpedon's comrade, Glaukos, sought out Hector, who was fighting in another part of the battlefield, and he spoke to him reproachfully. 'Hector,' he said, 'art thou utterly forgetful of those who came from their own country to help thee to

protect thy father's City? Sarpedon has fallen, and Achilles' Myrmidons would strip him of his armor and bring his body to the ships that their triumph over him may be greater still. Disgraceful will it be to thee, Hector, if they win that triumph.'

"Hector, when this was said to him, did not delay, but came straight to the spot where Sarpedon had been slain. The Greek who had laid hands upon the body he instantly slew. But as he fought on it suddenly seemed to Hector that the gods had resolved to give victory to the Greeks, and his spirit grew weary and hopeless within him. He turned his horses' heads toward the City and galloped from the press of battle. Then the Trojans who were fighting round it fled from the body of Sarpedon, and the Greeks took it and stripped it of its armor and carried the body to their ships.

"It was then that Patroklos forgot the command of Achilles — the command that he was not to bring the battle beyond the ships and that he was to return when the Trojans were beaten toward their City. Patroklos forgot all that, and he shouted to the immortal horses, Xanthos and Balios, that drew his chariot, and, slaying warrior after warrior he swept across the plain and came to the very gates of Troy.

"Now Hector was within the gates and had not yet left his chariot. Then there came and stood before him one who was thought to be the god Apollo, but who then had the likeness of a mortal man. 'Hector,' said he, 'why hast thou ceased from the fight? Behold, Patroklos is without

the gate of thy father's City. Turn thy horses against him now and strive to slay him, and may the gods give thee glory.'

"Then Hector bade his charioteer drive his horses through the gate and into the press of battle. He drew near to Patroklos, and Patroklos, leaping down from his chariot, seized a great stone and flung it at Hector's charioteer. It struck him on the brow and hurled him from the chariot.

"Hector too leaped from the chariot and took his sword in hand. Their men joined Patroklos and joined Hector and the battle began beside the body of Hector's charioteer. Three times did Patroklos rush against the ranks of the Trojans and nine warriors did he slay at each onset. But the doom of Patroklos was nigh. A warrior smote him in the back and struck the helmet from his head. With its high horse-hair crest it rolled beneath the hooves of the horses. Who was it smote Prince Patroklos then? Men said it was the god Apollo who would not have the sacred City of Troy taken until the time the gods had willed it to fall.

"The spear fell from his hands, the great shield that Achilles had given him dropped on the ground, and all in amaze Patroklos stood. He gave ground and retreated toward his comrades. Then did Hector deal him the stroke that slew. With his great spear he struck and drove it through the body of Patroklos.

"Then did Hector exult crying, 'Patroklos, thou didst swear that thou wouldst sack our sacred City and that thou wouldst take from our people their day of freedom. Now thou hast fallen and Our City need not dread thee ever any more!'

"Then said Patroklos, 'Thou mayst boast now, Hector, although it was not thy stroke that slew me. Apollo's stroke it was that sent me down. Boast of my slaying as thou wilt, but hear my saying and keep it in thy heart: Thy fate too is measured and thee Achilles will slay.'

"But Hector did not heed what the dying Patroklos said. He took from his body the armor of Achilles that had been a gift from the gods. The body too he would have brought within the City that his triumph might be greater, but now Aias came to where Patroklos had fallen and over the body he placed his great shield. The fight went on and Hector, withdrawing himself to the plain, put upon himself the armor he had stripped off the body of Patroklos. The armor fitted every limb and joint and as he put it on more courage and strength than ever yet he had felt came into the soul of Hector.

"And the immortal steeds that Patroklos had driven, having galloped from the battle, stood apart and would not move for all that their charioteer would do. They stood apart with their heads bowed, and tears flowed from their eyes down on the ground. And Zeus, the greatest of the gods, saw them and had pity upon them and spoke to himself saying, 'Ah, immortal steeds, why did I give ye to king Peleus, whose generations die while ye remain young and undying? Was it that ye should know the sorrows that befall mortal men? Pitiful, indeed, is the lot of all men upon the earth. Even Hector now, who boasteth in the armor that the gods once gave, will shortly go down to his death and the City he defendeth will be burned with fire.'

"So saying he put courage into the hearts of the immortal steeds and they went where the charioteer would have them go, and they came safely out of the battle.

"Now Hector, with the armor of Achilles upon him, gathered his companies together and brought them up to the battle to win and carry away the body of Patroklos. But each one who laid hands upon that body was instantly slain by Aias. All day the battle went on, for the Greeks would say to each other, 'Comrades, let the earth yawn and swallow us rather than let the Trojans carry off the body of Patroklos.' And on their side the Trojans would say, 'Friends, rather let us all be slain together beside this man than let one of us go backward now.'

"Now Nestor's son, Antilochos, who was fighting on the left of the battlefield, heard of the slaying of Patroklos. His eyes filled with tears and his voice was choked with grief and he dashed out of the battle to bring the grievous tidings to the hut of Achilles. 'Fallen is Patroklos,' he cried, 'and Greeks and Trojans are fighting around his body. And his body is naked now, for Hector has stripped the armor from it.'

"Then Achilles fainted away, and his head lay in the ashes of his hut. He woke again and moaned terribly. His goddess-mother heard the sound of his grief as she sat within the depths of the Ocean. She came to him as he was still moaning terribly. She took his hand and clasped it and said, 'My child, why weep'st thou?' Achilles ceased his moaning and answered, 'Patroklos, my dear friend, has been slain. Now I shall have no joy in my life save the joy of slaying Hector who slew my friend.'

"Thetis, his goddess-mother, wept when she heard such speech from Achilles. 'Shortlived you will be, my son,' she said, 'for it is appointed by the gods that after the death of Hector your death will come.'

" 'Straightway then let me die,' said Achilles, 'since I let my friend die without giving him help. O that I had not let my wrath overcome my spirit! Here I stayed, a useless burthen on the earth, while my comrades and my own dear friend fought for their country — here I stayed, I who am the best of all the Greeks. But now let me go into the battle and let the Trojans know that Achilles has come back, although he tarried long.'

" 'But thine armor, my son,' said Thetis. 'Thou hast no armor now to protect thee in the battle. Go not into it until thou seest me again. In the morning I shall return and I shall bring thee armor that Hephaistos, the smith of the gods, shall make for thee.'

"So she spoke, and she turned from her son, and she went to Olympus where the gods have their dwellings.

"Now darkness had come down on those who battled round the body of Patroklos, and in that darkness more Greeks than Trojans were slain. It seemed to the Greeks that Zeus had resolved to give the victory to the Trojans and not to them, and they were dismayed. But four Greek

heroes lifted up the body and put it upon their shoulders, and Aias and his brother stood facing the Trojans, holding them back while the four tried to bear the body away. The Trojans pressed on, striking with swords and axes, but like a wooded ridge that stretches across a plain and holds back a mighty flood, Aias and his brother held their ground.

"Achilles still lay in his hut, moaning in his grief, and the servants raised loud lamentations outside the hut. The day wore on and the battle went on and Hector strove against Aias and his brother. Then the figure of a goddess appeared before Achilles as he lay on the ground. 'Rouse thee, Achilles,' she said, 'or Hector will drag into Troy the body of thy friend, Patroklos.'

"Said Achilles, 'Goddess Iris, how may I go into the battle since the Trojans hold the armor that should protect me?'

"Said Iris, the Messenger of the gods, 'Go down to the wall as thou art and show thyself to the men of Troy, and it may be that they will shrink back on seeing thee and hearing thy voice, and so give those who defend the body of Patroklos a breathing-spell.'

"So she said and departed. Then Achilles arose and went down to the wall that had been built around the ships. He stood upon the wall and shouted across the trench, and friends and foes saw him and heard his voice. Around his head a flame of fire arose such as was never seen before around the head of a mortal man. And seeing the flame of fire around his head and hearing his terrible voice the Trojans were affrighted and stood still. Then the Greeks took up the body of Patroklos and laid it on a litter and bore it out of the battle."

XVI

NOW Thetis, the mother of Achilles, went to Olympus where the gods have their dwellings and to the house of Hephaistos, the smith of the gods. That house shone above all the houses on Olympus because Hephaistos himself had made it of shining bronze. And inside the house there were wonders — handmaidens that were not living but that were made out of gold and made with such wondrous skill that they waited upon Hephaistos and served and helped him as though they were living maids.

"Hephaistos was lame and crooked of foot and went limping. He and Thetis were friends from of old time, for, when his mother would have forsaken him because of his crooked foot, Thetis and her sister reared him within one of the Ocean's caves and it was while he was with them that he began to work in metals. So the lame god was pleased to see Thetis in his dwelling and he welcomed her and clasped her hand and asked of her what she would have him do for her.

"Then Thetis, weeping, told him of her son Achilles, how he had lost his dear friend and how he was moved to go into the battle to fight with Hector, and how he was without armor to protect his life, seeing that the armor that the gods had once given his father was now in the hands of his foe. And Thetis besought Hephaistos to make new armor for her son that he might go into the battle.

"She no sooner finished speaking than Hephaistos went to his work-bench and set his bellows — twenty were there — working. And the twenty bellows blew into the crucibles and made bright and hot fires. Then Hephaistos threw into the fires bronze and tin and silver and gold. He set on the anvil-stand a great anvil, and took in one hand his hammer and in the other hand his tongs.

"For the armor of Achilles he made first a shield and then a corselet that gleamed like fire. And he made a strong helmet to go on the head and shining greaves to wear on the ankles. The shield was made with five folds, one fold of metal upon the other, so that it was so strong and thick that no spear or arrow could pierce it. And upon this shield he hammered out images that were a wonder to men.

"The first were images of the sun and the moon and of the stars that the shepherds and the seamen watch — the Pleiades and Hyads and Orion and the Bear that is also called the Wain. And below he hammered out the images of two cities: in one there were people going to feasts and playing music and dancing and giving judgments in the market-place: the other was a city besieged: there were warriors on the walls and there was an army marching out of the gate to give battle to those that besieged them. And

below the images of the cities he made a picture of a ploughed field, with ploughmen driving their yokes of oxen along the furrows, and with men bringing them cups of wine. And he made a picture of another field where men were reaping and boys were gathering the corn, where there was a servant beneath an oak tree making ready a feast, and women making ready barley for a supper for the men who were reaping, and a King standing apart and watching all, holding a staff in his hands and rejoicing at all he saw.

"And another image he made of a vineyard, with clusters of grapes that showed black, and with the vines hanging from silver poles. And he showed maidens and youths in the vineyard, gathering the grapes into baskets, and one amongst them, a boy, who played on the viol. Beside the image of the vineyard he made images of cattle, with herdsmen, and with nine dogs guarding them. But he showed two lions that had come up and had seized the bull of the herd, and the dogs and men strove to drive them away but were affrighted. And beside the image of the oxen he made the image of a pasture land, with sheep in it, and sheepfolds and roofed huts.

"He made yet another picture — a dancing-place with youths and maidens dancing, their hands upon each others' hands. Beautiful dresses and wreaths of flowers the maidens had on, and the youths had daggers of gold hanging from their silver belts. A great company stood around those who were dancing, and amongst them there was a minstrel who played on the lyre.

"Then all around the rim of the shield Hephaistos, the lame god, set an image of Ocean, whose stream goes round the world. Not long was he in making the shield and the other wonderful pieces of armor. As soon as the armor was ready Thetis put her hands upon it, and flying down from Olympus like a hawk, brought it to the feet of Achilles, her son.

"And Achilles, when he saw the splendid armor that Hephaistos the lame god had made for him, rose up from where he lay and took the wonderfully wrought piece in his hands. And he began to put the armor upon him, and none of the Myrmidons who were around could bear to look upon it, because it shone with such brightness and because it had all the marks of being the work of a god."

XVII

THEN Achilles put his shining armor upon him and it fitted him as though it were wings; he put the wonderful shield before him and he took in his hands the great spear that Cheiron the Centaur had given to Peleus his father — that spear that no one else but Achilles could wield. He bade his charioteer harness the immortal horses Xanthos and Balios. Then as he mounted his chariot Achilles spoke to the horses, 'Xanthos and Balios,' he said, 'this time bring the hero that goes with you back safely to the ships, and do

not leave him dead on the plain as ye left the hero Patroklos.'

"Then Xanthos the immortal steed spoke, answering
for himself and his comrade. 'Achilles,' he said, with his
head bowed and his mane touching the ground, 'Achilles,
for this time we will bring thee safely back from the battle. But a day will come when we shall not bring thee
back, when thou too shalt lie with the dead before the
walls of Troy.'

"Then was Achilles troubled and he said, 'Xanthos, my
steed, why dost thou remind me by thy prophecies of what
I know already — that my death too is appointed, and that
I am to perish here, far from my father and my mother
and my own land.'

"Then he drove his immortal horses into the battle.
The Trojans were affrighted when they saw Achilles himself in the fight, blazing in the armor that Hephaistos had
made for him. They went backward before his onset. And
Achilles shouted to the captains of the Greeks, 'No longer
stand apart from the men of Troy, but go with me into
the battle and let each man throw his whole soul into the
fight.'

"And on the Trojan side Hector cried to his captains
and said, 'Do not let Achilles drive you before him. Even
though his hands are as irresistible as fire and his fierce-
ness as terrible as flashing steel, I shall go against him and
face him with my spear.'

"But Achilles went on, and captain after captain of the
Trojans went down before him. Now amongst the war-

riors whom he caught sight of in the fight was Polydoros, the brother of Hector and the youngest of all King Priam's sons. Priam forbade him ever to go into the battle because he loved him as he would love a little child. But Polydoros had gone in this day, trusting to his fleetness of foot to escape with his life. Achilles saw him and pursued him and slew him with the spear. Hector saw the death of his brother. Then he could no longer endure to stand aside to order the battle. He came straight up to where Achilles was brandishing his great spear. And when Achilles saw Hector before him he cried out, 'Here is the man who most deeply wounded my soul, who slew my dear friend Patroklos. Now shall we two fight each other and Patroklos shall be avenged by me.' And he shouted to Hector, 'Now Hector, the day of thy triumph and the day of thy life is at its end.'

"But Hector answered him without fear, 'Not with words, Achilles, can you affright me. Yet I know that thou art a man of might and a stronger man than I. But the fight between us depends upon the will of the gods. I shall do my best against thee, and my spear before this has been found to have a dangerous edge.'

"He spoke and lifted up his spear and flung it at Achilles. Then the breath of a god turned Hector's spear aside, for it was not appointed that either he or Achilles should be then slain. Achilles darted at Hector to slay him with his spear. But a god hid Hector from Achilles in a thick mist.

"Then in a rage Achilles drove his chariot into the

ranks of the war and many great captains he slew. He came to Skamandros, the river that flows across the plain before the city of Troy. And so many men did he slay in it that the river rose in anger against him for choking its waters with the bodies of men.

"Then on toward the City, he went like a fire raging through a glen that had been parched with heat. Now on a tower of the walls of Troy, Priam the old King stood, and he saw the Trojans coming in a rout toward the City, and he saw Achilles in his armor blazing like a star — like that star that is seen at harvest time and is called Orion's Dog; the star that is the brightest of all stars, but yet is a sign of evil. And the old man Priam sorrowed greatly as he stood upon the tower and watched Achilles, because he knew in his heart whom this man would slay — Hector, his son, the protector of his City."

XVIII

SO much of the story of Achilles did Telemachus, the son of Odysseus, hear from the lips of King Menelaus as he sat with his comrade Peisistratus in the King's feasting-hall. And more would Menelaus have told them then if Helen, his wife, had not been seen to weep. "Why weepst thou, Helen?" said Menelaus. "Ah, surely I know. It is because the words that tell of the death of Hector are sorrowful to thee."

And Helen, the lovely lady, said "Never did Prince Hector speak a hard or a harsh word to me in all the years I was in his father's house. And if anyone upbraided me he would come and speak gentle words to me. Ah, greatly did I lament for the death of noble Hector! After his wife and his mother I wept the most for him. And when one speaks of his slaying I cannot help but weep."

Said Menelaus, "Relieve your heart of its sorrow, Helen, by praising Hector to this youth and by telling your memories of him."

"Tomorrow I shall do so," said the lady Helen. She went with her maids from the hall and the servants took Telemachus and Peisistratus to their sleeping places.

The next day they sat in the banqueting hall; King Menelaus and Telemachus and Peisistratus, and the lady Helen came amongst them. Her handmaidens brought into the hall her silver workbasket that had wheels beneath it with rims of gold, and her golden distaff that, with the basket, had been presents from the wife of the King of Egypt. And Helen sat in her chair and took the distaff in her hands and worked on the violet-colored wool that was in her basket. And as she worked she told Telemachus of Troy and of its guardian, Hector.

Said Helen, "The old men were at the gate of the City talking over many things, and King Priam was amongst them. It was in the days when Achilles first quarrelled with King Agamemnon. 'Come hither, my daughter,' said King Priam to me, 'and sit by me and tell me who the warriors are who now come out upon the plain. You have seen them all before, and I would have you tell me who such and such a one is. Who is yon hero who seems so mighty? I have seen men who were more tall then he by a head, but I have never seen a man who looked more royal.'

"I said to King Priam. 'The hero whom you look upon is the leader of the host of the Greeks. He is the renowned King Agamemnon.'

" 'He looks indeed a King,' said Priam. 'Tell me now who the other warrior is who is shorter by a head than King Agamemnon, but who is broader of chest and shoulder.'

" 'He is Odysseus,' I said, 'who was reared in rugged Ithaka, but who is wise above all the Kings.'

"And an old man, Antenor, who was by us said, 'That indeed is Odysseus. I remember that he and Menelaus came on an embassy to the assembly of the Trojans. When they both stood up, Menelaus seemed the greater man, but when they sat down Odysseus seemed by far the more stately. When they spoke in the assembly, Menelaus was ready and skilful of speech. Odysseus when he spoke held his staff stiffly in his hands and fixed his eyes on the ground. We thought by the look of him then that he was a man of no understanding. But when he began to speak we saw that no one could match Odysseus — his words came like snowflakes in winter and his voice was very resonant.'

"And Priam said, 'Who is that huge warrior? I think he is taller and broader than any of the rest.'

" 'He is great Aias,' I said, 'who is as a bulwark for the Greeks. And beside him stands Idomeneus, who has come from the Island of Crete. Around him stand the Cretan captains.' So I spoke, but my heart was searching for a sight of my own two brothers. I did not see them in any of the companies. Had they come with the host, I wondered, and were they ashamed to be seen with the warriors on account of my wrongdoing? I wondered as I looked for them. Ah, I did not know that even then my two dear brothers were dead, and that the earth of their own dear land held them.

"Hector came to the gate and the wives and daughters of the Trojans came running to him, asking for news of their husbands or sons or brothers, whether they were killed or whether they were coming back from the battle. He spoke to them all and went to his own house. But Andromache, his wife, was not there, and the housedame told him that she had gone to the great tower by the wall of the City to watch the battle and that the nurse had gone with her, bringing their infant child.

"So Hector went down the street and came to the gate where we were, and Andromache his wife came to meet him. With her was the nurse who carried the little child that the folk of the city named Astyanax, calling him 'King of the City' because his father was their city's pro tector. Hector stretched out his arms to the little boy whom the nurse carried. But the child shrank away from him, because he was frightened of the great helmet on his father's head with its horse-hair crest. Then Hector laughed and Andromache laughed with him, and Hector took off his great helmet and laid it on the ground. Then he took up his little son and dandled him in his arms, and prayed, 'O Zeus, greatest of the gods, grant that this son of mine may become valiant, and that, like me, he may be protector of the City and thereafter a great King, so that men may say of him as he returns from battle, 'Far greater is he than was Hector his father.' Saying this he left the child back in his nurse's arms. And to Andromache, his wife, who that day was very fearful, he said 'Dear one, do not be oversorrowful. You urge me not to go every day into the battle, but some days to stay behind the walls. But my own spirit forbids me to stay away from battle, for always I have taught myself to be valiant and to fight in the forefront.'

"So he said and he put on his helmet again and went to order his men. And his wife went toward the house, looking back at him often and letting her tears fall down. Thou knowst from Menelaus' story what triumphs Hector had thereafter — how he drove the Greeks back to their ships and affrighted them with his thousand watchfires upon the plain; how he drove back the host that Agamemnon led when Diomedes and Odysseus and Machaon the healer were wounded; how he broke through the wall that the Greeks had builded and brought fire to their ships, and how he slew Patroklos in the armor of Achilles."

XIX

KING Priam on his tower saw Achilles come raging across the plain and he cried out to Hector, 'Hector, beloved son, do not await this man's onset but come within the City's walls. Come within that thou mayst live and be a protection to the men and women of Troy. And come within that thou mayst save my father who must perish if thou art slain.'

"But Hector would not come within the walls of the City. He stood holding his shield against a jutting tower in the wall. And all around him were the Trojans, who came pouring in through the gate without waiting to speak to each other to ask who were yet living and who were slain. And as he stood there he was saying in his heart, 'The fault is mine that the Trojans have been defeated upon the plain. I kept them from entering the City last night against the counsel of a wise man, for in my pride I thought it would be easy to drive Achilles and the Greeks back again and defeat them utterly and destroy their hopes of return. Now are the Trojans defeated and dishonored and many have lost their lives through my pride. Now the women of Troy will say, 'Hector, by trusting to his own might, has brought destruction upon the whole host and our husbands and sons and brothers have perished because of him.' Rather than hear them say this

I shall face Achilles and slay him and save the City, or, if it must be, perish by his spear.'

"When Achilles came near him Hector spoke to him and said 'My heart bids me stand against thee although thou art a mightier man than I. But before we go into battle let us take pledges, one from the other, with the gods to witness, that, if I should slay thee, I shall strip thee of thine armor but I shall not carry thy body into the City but shall give it to thine own friends to treat with all honor, and that, if thou should slay me, thou shalt give my body to my friends.'

"But Achilles said, 'Between me and thee there can be no pledges. Fight, and fight with all thy soldiership, for now I shall strive to make thee pay for all the sorrow thou hast brought to me because of the slaying of Patroklos, my friend.'

"He spoke and raised his spear and flung it. But with his quickness Hector avoided Achilles' spear. And he raised his own, saying, 'Thou hast missed me, and not yet is the hour of my doom. Now it is thy turn to stand before my spear.'

"He flung it, but the wonderful shield of Achilles turned Hector's spear and it fell on the ground. Then was Hector downcast, for he had no other spear. He drew his sword and sprang at Achilles. But the helmet and shield of Achilles let none of Hector's great strokes touch his body. And Achilles got back into his hands his own great spear, and he stood guarding himself with his shield and watching Hector for a spot to strike him on. Now in the armor that

Hector wore — the armor that he had stripped off Patroklos — there was a point at the neck where there was an
opening. As Hector came on Achilles drove at his neck
with his spear and struck him and Hector fell in the dust.

"Then Achilles stripped from him the armor that Patroklos had worn. The other captains of the Greeks came
up and looked at Hector where he lay and all marvelled
at his size and strength and goodliness. And Achilles
dragged the body at his chariot and drove away toward the
ships.

"Hector's mother, standing on the tower on the wall,
saw all that was done and she broke into a great cry. And
all the women of Troy took up the cry and wailed for
Prince Hector who had guarded them and theirs from the
foe. Andromache, his wife, did not know the terrible thing
that had happened. She was in an inner chamber of Hector's house, weaving a great web of cloth and broidering
it with flowers, and she had ordered her handmaidens to
heat water for the bath, so that Hector might refresh himself when he came in from the fight. But now she heard
the wail of the women of Troy. Fear came upon her, for
she knew that such wailing was for the best of their warriors.

"She ran from her chamber and out into the street and
came to the battlements where the people stood watching.
She saw the chariot of Achilles dashing off toward the
ships and she knew that it dragged the dead body of Hector. Then darkness came before her eyes and she fainted
away. Her husband's sisters and his brothers' wives

thronged round her and lifted her up. And at last her life came back to her and she wailed for Hector, 'O my husband,' she cried, 'for misery were we two born! Now thou hast been slain by Achilles and I am left husbandless! And ah, woe for our young child! Hard-hearted strangers shall oppress him when he lives amongst people that care not for him or his. And he will come weeping to me, his widowed mother, who will live forever sorrowful thinking upon where thou liest, Hector, by the ships of those who slew thee.'

"So Andromache spoke and all the women of Troy joined in her grief and wept for great Hector who had protected their city."

XX

NOW that Hector was dead, King Priam, his father, had only one thought in his mind, and that was to get his body from Achilles and bring it into the City so that it might be treated with the honor befitting the man who had been the guardian of Troy. And while he sat in his grief, thinking of his noble son lying so far from those who would have wept over him, behold! There appeared before him Iris, the messenger of Zeus, the greatest of the Gods. Iris said to him, 'King, thou mayst ransom from Achilles the body of Hector, thy noble son. Go thou thyself to the hut of Achilles and bring with thee great gifts to offer him. Take with thee a wagon that thou mayst bring back in it the body, and let only one old henchman go with thee to drive the mules.'

"Then Priam, when he heard this, arose and went into his treasure chamber and took out of his chests twelve beautiful robes; twelve bright-colored cloaks; twelve soft coverlets and ten talents of gold; he took, too, four cauldrons and two tripods and a wonderful goblet that the men of Thrace had given him when they had come on an embassy to his city. Then he called upon his sons and he bade them make ready the wagon and load it with the treasures he had brought out of his treasure chamber.

"When the wagon was loaded and the mules were yoked under it, and when Priam and his henchman had mounted the seats, Hekabe, the queen, Priam's wife and the mother of Hector, came with wine and with a golden cup that they might pour out an offering to the gods before they went on their journey; that they might know whether the gods indeed favored it, or whether Priam himself was not going into danger. King Priam took the cup from his wife and he poured out wine from it, and looking toward heaven he prayed, 'O Father Zeus, grant that I may find welcome under Achilles' roof, and send, if thou wilt, a bird of omen, so that seeing it with mine own eyes I may go on my way trusting that no harm will befall me.'

"He prayed, and straightway a great eagle was seen with wide wings spread out above the City, and when they saw the eagle, the hearts of the people were glad for they knew that their King would come back safely and with the body of Prince Hector who had guarded Troy.

"Now Priam and his henchman drove across the plain of Troy and came to the river that flowed across and there they let their mules drink. They were greatly troubled, for dark night was coming down and they knew not the way to the hut of Achilles. They were in fear too that some company of armed men would come upon them and slay them for the sake of the treasures they had in the wagon.

"The henchman saw a young man coming toward them. And when he reached them he spoke to them kindly and offered to guide them through the camp and to the hut of Achilles. He mounted the wagon and took the reins in his hands and drove the mules. He brought them to the hut of Achilles and helped Priam from the wagon and carried the gifts they had brought within the hut. 'Know, King Priam,' he said, 'that I am not a mortal, but that I am one sent by Zeus to help and companion thee upon the way. Go now within the hut and speak to Achilles and ask him, for his father's sake, to restore to thee the body of Hector, thy son.'

"So he spoke and departed and King Priam went within the hut. There great Achilles was sitting and King Priam went to him and knelt before him and clasped the hands of the man who had slain his son. And Achilles wondered when he saw him there, for he did not know how one could have come to his hut and entered it without being seen. He knew then that it was one of the gods who had

guided this man. Priam spoke to him and said, 'Bethink thee, Achilles upon thine own father. He is now of an age with me, and perhaps even now, in thy faraway country, there are those who make him suffer pain and misery. But however great the pain and misery he may suffer he is happy compared to me, for he knows that thou, his son, art still alive. But I no longer have him who was the best of my sons. Now for thy father's sake have I come to thee, Achilles, to ask for the body of Hector, my son. I am more pitiable than thy father or than any man, for I have come through dangers to take in my hands the hands that slew my son.'

"Achilles remembered his father and felt sorrow for the old man who knelt before him. He took King Priam by the hand and raised him up and seated him on the bench beside him. And he wept, remembering old Peleus, his father.

"He called his handmaids and he bade them take the body of Hector and wash it and wrap it in two of the robes that Priam had brought. When they had done all this he took up the body of Hector and laid it himself upon the wagon.

"Then he came and said to King Priam, 'Thy son is laid upon a bier, and at the break of day thou mayst bring him back to the City. But now eat and rest here for this night.'

"King Priam ate, and he looked at Achilles and he saw how great and how goodly he was. And Achilles looked at Priam and he saw how noble and how kingly he looked.

And this was the first time that Achilles and Priam the King of Troy really saw each other.

"When they gazed on each other King Priam said, 'When thou goest to lie down, lord Achilles, permit me to lie down also. Not once have my eyelids closed in sleep since my son Hector lost his life. And now I have tasted bread and meat and wine for the first time since, and I could sleep.'

"Achilles ordered that a bed be made in the portico for King Priam and his henchman, but before they went Achilles said: 'Tell me, King, and tell me truly, for how many days dost thou desire to make a funeral for Hector? For so many days space I will keep back the battle from the City so that thou mayst make the funeral in peace.' 'For nine days we would watch beside Hector's body and lament for him; on the tenth day we would have the funeral; on the eleventh day we would make the barrow over him, and on the twelfth day we would fight,' King Priam said. 'Even for twelve days I will hold the battle back from the City,' said Achilles.

"Then Priam and his henchman went to rest. But in the middle of the night the young man who had guided him to the hut of Achilles — the god Hermes he was — appeared before his bed and bade him rise and go to the wagon and yoke the mules and drive back to the City with the body of Hector. Priam aroused his henchman and they went out and yoked the mules and mounted the wagon, and with Hermes to guide them they drove back to the City.

"And Achilles on his bed thought of his own fate — how he too would die in battle, and how for him there would be no father to make lament. But he would be laid where he had asked his friends to lay him — beside Patroklos — and over them both the Greeks would raise a barrow that would be wondered at in aftertimes.

"So Achilles thought. And afterwards the arrow fired by Paris struck him as he fought before the gate of the City, and he was slain even on the place where he slew Hector. But the Greeks carried off his body and his armor and brought them back to the ships. And Achilles was lamented over, though not by old Peleus, his father. From the depths of the sea came Thetis, his goddess-mother, and with her came the Maidens of the Sea. They covered the body of Achilles with wonderful raiment and over it they lamented for seventeen days and seventeen nights. On the eighteenth day he was laid in the grave beside Patroklos, his dear friend, and over them both the Greeks raised a barrow that was wondered at in the aftertimes."

XXI

NOW Hector's sister was the first to see her father coming in the dawn across the plain of Troy with the wagon upon which his body was laid. She came down to the City and she cried through the streets, 'O men and women of Troy, ye who often went to the gates to meet Hector coming back with victory, come now to the gates to receive Hector dead.'

"Then every man and woman in the City took themselves outside the gate. And they brought in the wagon upon which Hector was laid, and all day from the early dawn to the going down of the sun they wailed for him who had been the guardian of their city.

"His father took the body to the house where Hector had lived and he laid it upon his bed. Then Hector's wife, Andromache, went to the bed and cried over the body. 'Husband,' she cried, 'thou art gone from life, and thou hast left me a widow in thy house. Our child is yet little, and he shall not grow to manhood in the halls that were thine, for long before that the City will be taken and destroyed. Ah, how can it stand, when thou, who wert its best guardian, hast perished? The folk lament thee, Hector; but for me and for thy little son, doomed to grow up amongst strangers and men unfriendly to him, the pain for thy death will ever abide.'

"And Hekabe, Hector's mother, went to the bed and cried 'Of all my children thou, Hector, wert the dearest. Thou wert slain because it was not thy way to play the coward; ever wert thou championing the men and women of Troy without thought of taking shelter or flight. And for that thou wert slain, my son.'

"And I, Helen, went to the bed too, to lament for noble Hector. 'Of all the friends I had in Troy, thou wert the dearest, Hector,' I cried. 'Never did I hear one harsh word from thee to me who brought wars and troubles to thy

City. In every way thou wert as a brother to me. Therefore I bewail thee with pain at my heart, for in all Troy there is no one now who is friendly to me.'

"Then did the King and the folk of the City prepare for Hector's funeral. On the tenth day, weeping most bitter tears they bore brave Hector away. And they made a grave for him, and over the grave they put close-set stones, and over it all they raised a great barrow. On the eleventh day they feasted at King Priam's house, and on the twelfth day the battle began anew."

XXII

FOR many days Telemachus and his comrade Peisistratus stayed in the house of King Menelaus. On the evening before he departed Menelaus spoke to him of the famous deeds of his father, Odysseus.

"Now Achilles was dead," said Menelaus, "and his glorious armor was offered as a prize for the warrior whom the Greeks thought the most of. Two men strove for the prize — Odysseus and his friend Aias. To Odysseus the armor of Achilles was given, but he was in no way glad of the prize, for his getting it had wounded the proud spirit of great Aias.

"It was fitting that Odysseus should have been given Achilles' armor, for no warrior in the host had done better than he. But Odysseus was to do still greater things for us. He knew that only one man could wield a bow better than Paris — Paris who had shot with an arrow Achilles, and who after that had slain many of our chiefs. That man was Philoctetes. He had come with Agamemnon's host to Troy. But Philoctetes had been bitten by a watersnake, and the wound given him was so terrible that none of our warriors could bear to be near him. He was left on the Island of Lemnos and the host lost memory of him. But Odysseus remembered, and he took ship to Lemnos and brought Philoctetes back. With his great bow and with the arrows of Hercules that were his, Philoctetes shot at Paris upon the wall of Troy and slew him with an arrow.

"And then Odysseus devised the means by which we took Priam's city at last. He made us build a great Wooden Horse. We built it and left it upon the plain of Troy and the Trojans wondered at it greatly. And Odysseus had counselled us to bring our ships down to the water and to burn our stores and make it seem in every way that we were going to depart from Troy in weariness. This we did, and the Trojans saw the great host sail away from before their City. But they did not know that a company of the best of our warriors was within the hollow of the Wooden Horse, nor did they know that we had left a spy behind to make a signal for our return.

"The Trojans wondered why the great Wooden Horse had been left behind. And there were some who considered that it had been left there as an offering to the goddess, Pallas Athene, and they thought it should be brought

within the city. Others were wiser and would have left the Wooden Horse alone. But those who considered that it should be brought within prevailed; and, as the Horse was too great to bring through the gate, they flung down part of the wall that they might bring it through. The Wooden Horse was brought within the walls and left upon the streets of the city and the darkness of the night fell.

"Now Helen, my wife, came down to where the Wooden Horse was, and she, suspecting there were armed men within, walked around it three times, calling to every captain of the Greeks who might be within in his own wife's voice. And when the sound of a voice that had not been heard for so many years came to him each of the captains started up to answer. But Odysseus put his hands across the mouth of each and so prevented them from being discovered.

"We had left a spy hidden between the beach and the city. Now when the Wooden Horse had been brought within the walls and night had fallen, the spy lighted a great fire that was signal to the ships that had sailed away. They returned with the host before the day broke. Then we who were within the Wooden Horse broke through the boards and came out on the City with our spears and swords in our hands. The guards beside the gates we slew and we made a citadel of the Wooden Horse and fought around it. The warriors from the ships crossed the wall where it was broken down, and we swept through the streets and came to the citadel of the King. Thus we took

Priam's City and all its treasures, and thus I won back my own wife, the lovely Helen.

"But after we had taken and sacked King Priam's City, great troubles came upon us. Some of us sailed away, and some of us remained on the shore at the bidding of King Agamemnon, to make sacrifice to the gods. We separated, and the doom of death came to many of us. Nestor I saw at Lesbos, but none other of our friends have I ever since seen. Agamemnon, my own brother, came to his own land. But ah, it would have been happier for him if he had died on the plain of Troy, and if we had left a great barrow heaped above him! For he was slain in his own house and by one who had married the wife he had left behind. When the Ancient One of the Sea told me of my brother's doom I sat down upon the sand and wept, and I was minded to live no more nor to see the light of the sun.

"And of thy father, Telemachus, I have told thee what I myself know and what was told me of him by the Ancient One of the Sea — how he stays on an Island where the nymph Calypso holds him against his will: but where that Island lies I do not know. Odysseus is there, and he cannot win back to his own country, seeing that he has no ship and no companions to help him to make his way across the sea. But Odysseus was ever master of devices. And also he is favored greatly by the goddess, Pallas Athene. For these reasons, Telemachus, be hopeful that your father will yet reach his own home and country."

XXIII

NOW the goddess, Pallas Athene, had thought for Telemachus, and she came to him where he lay in the vestibule of Menelaus' house. His comrade, Peisistratus was alseep, but Telemachus was wakeful, thinking upon his father.

Athene stood before his bed and said to him, "Telemachus, no longer shouldst thou wander abroad, for the time has come when thou shouldst return. Come. Rouse Menelaus, and let him send thee upon thy way."

Then Telemachus woke Peisistratus out of his sleep and told him that it was best that they should be going on their journey. But Peisistratus said, "Tarry until it is dawn, Telemachus, when Menelaus will come to us and send us on our way."

Then when it was light King Menelaus came to them. When he heard that they would depart he told the lady Helen to bid the maids prepare a meal for them. He himself, with Helen, his wife, and Megapenthes, his son, went down into his treasure chamber and brought forth for gifts to Telemachus a two-handled cup and a great mixing bowl of silver. And Helen took out of a chest a beautiful robe that she herself had made and embroidered. They came to Telemachus where he stood by the chariot with Peisistratus ready to depart. Then Menelaus gave him the beautiful two-handled cup that had been a gift to himself from the king of the Sidonians. Megapenthes brought up the great bowl of silver and put it in the chariot, and beautiful Helen came to him holding the embroidered robe.

"I too have a gift, dear child, for thee," she said. "Bring this robe home and leave it in thy mother's keeping. I want thee to have it to give to thy bride when thou bringest her into thy father's halls."

Then were the horses yoked to the chariot and Telemachus and Peisistratus bade farewell to Menelaus and Helen who had treated them so kindly. As they were ready to go Menelaus poured out of a golden cup wine as an offering to the gods. And as Menelaus poured it out, Telemachus prayed that he might find Odysseus, his father, in his home.

Now as he prayed a bird flew from the right hand and over the horses' heads. It was an eagle, and it bore in its claws a goose that belonged to the farmyard. Telemachus asked Menelaus was this not a sign from Zeus, the greatest of the Gods.

Then said Helen, "Hear me now, for I will prophesy from this sign to you. Even as yonder eagle has flown down from the mountain and killed a goose of the farmyard, so will Odysseus come from far to his home and kill the wooers who are there."

"May Zeus grant that it be so," said Telemachus. He spoke and lashed the horses, and they sped across the plain.

When they came near the city of Pylos, Telemachus spoke to his comrade, Peisistratus, and said:

"Do not take me past my ship, son of Nestor. Thy good father expects me to return to his house, but I fear that if I should, he, out of friendliness, would be anxious to make me stay many days. But I know that I should now return to Ithaka."

The son of Nestor turned the horses toward the sea and they drove the chariot to where Telemachus' ship was anchored. Then Telemachus gathered his followers, and he bade them take on board the presents that Menelaus and Helen had given him.

They did this, and they raised the mast and the sails and the rowers took their seats on the benches. A breeze came and the sails took it and Telemachus and his companions sailed toward home. And all unknown to the youth, his father, Odysseus, was even then nearing his home.

PART II

How Odysseus left Calypso's island and came to the land
of the Phaeacians; how he told he fared with the Cyclopes
and went past the terrible Scylla and Charybdis and came
to the island of Thrinacia where his men slaughtered the
cattle of the sun; how he was given a ship by the Phaeacians and came to his own land; how he overthrew the
wooers who wasted his substance and came to reign again
as king of Ithaka

I

EVER mindful was Pallas Athene of Odysseus although she might not help him openly because of a wrong he had done Poseidon, the god of the sea. But she spoke at the council of the gods, and she won from Zeus a pledge that Odysseus would now be permitted to return to his own land. On that day she went to Ithaka, and, appearing to Telemachus, moved him, as has been told, to go on the voyage in search of his father. And on that day, too, Hermes, by the will of Zeus, went to Ogygia — to that Island where, as the Ancient One of the Sea had shown Menelaus, Odysseus was held by the nymph Calypso.

Beautiful indeed was that Island. All round the cave where Calypso lived was a blossoming wood — alder, poplar and cypress trees were there, and on their branches roosted long-winged birds — falcons and owls and chattering sea-crows. Before the cave was a soft meadow in which thousands of violets bloomed, and with four fountains that gushed out of the ground and made clear streams through the grass. Across the cave grew a straggling vine, heavy with clusters of grapes. Calypso was within the cave, and as Hermes came near, he heard her singing one of her magic songs.

She was before a loom weaving the threads with a golden shuttle. Now she knew Hermes and was pleased to see him on her Island, but as soon as he spoke of Odysseus and how it was the will of Zeus that he should be permitted to leave the Island, her song ceased and the golden shuttle fell from her hand.

"Woe to me," she said, "and woe to any immortal who loves a mortal, for the gods are always jealous of their love. I do not hold him here because I hate Odysseus, but because I love him greatly, and would have him dwell with me here — more than this, Hermes, I would make him an immortal so that he would know neither old age nor death."

"He does not desire to be freed from old age and death," said Hermes. "He desires to return to his own land and to live with his dear wife, Penelope, and his son, Telemachus. And Zeus, the greatest of the gods, commands that you let him go upon his way."

"I have no ship to give him," said Calypso, "and I have no company of men to help him to cross the sea."

"He must leave the Island and cross the sea — Zeus commands it," Hermes said.

"I must help him to make his way across the sea if it must be so," Calypso said. Then she bowed her head and Hermes went from her.

Straightway Calypso left her cave and went down to the sea. By the shore Odysseus stayed, looking across the wide sea with tears in his eyes.

She came to him and she said, "Be not sorrowful any more, Odysseus. The time has come when thou mayst depart from my Island. Come now. I will show how I can help thee on thy way."

She brought him to the side of the Island where great trees grew and she put in his hands a double-edged axe and an adze. Then Odysseus started to hew down the timber. Twenty trees he felled with his axe of bronze, and he smoothed them and made straight the line. Calypso came to him at the dawn of the next day; she brought augers for boring and he made the beams fast. He built a raft, making it very broad, and set a mast upon it and fixed a rudder to guide it. To make it more secure, he wove out of osier rods a fence that went from stem to stern as a bulwark against the waves, and he strengthened the bulwark with wood placed behind. Calypso wove him a web of cloth for sails, and these he made very skilfully. Then he fastened the braces and the halyards and sheets, and he pushed the raft with levers down to the sea.

That was on the fourth day. On the fifth Calypso gave him garments for the journey and brought provision down to the raft — two skins of wine and a great skin of water; corn and many dainties. She showed Odysseus how to guide his course by the star that some call the Bear and others the Wain, and she bade farewell to him. He took his place on the raft and set his sail to the breeze and he sailed away from Ogygia, the island where Calypso had held him for so long.

But not easily or safely did he make his way across the sea. The winds blew upon his raft and the waves dashed against it; a fierce blast came and broke the mast in the middle; the sail and the yardarm fell into the deep. Then Odysseus was flung down on the bottom of the raft. For a long time he lay there overwhelmed by the water that broke over him. The winds drove the raft to and fro — the South wind tossed it to the North to bear along, and the East wind tossed it to the West to chase.

In the depths of the sea there was a Nymph who saw his toils and his troubles and who had pity upon him. Ino was her name. She rose from the waves in the likeness of a seagull and she sat upon the raft and she spoke to Odysseus in words.

"Hapless man," she said, "Poseidon, the god of the sea, is still wroth with thee. It may be that the waters will destroy the raft upon which thou sailest. Then there would be no hope for thee. But do what I bid thee and thou shalt yet escape. Strip off thy garments and take this veil from me and wind it around thy breast. As long as it is upon thee thou canst not drown. But when thou reachest the mainland loose the veil and cast it into the sea so that it may come back to me."

She gave him the veil, and then, in the likeness of a seagull, she dived into the sea and the waves closed over her. Odysseus took the veil and wound it around his breast, but he would not leave the raft as long as its timbers held together.

Then a great wave came and shattered the raft. He held himself on a single beam as one holds himself on a horse, and then, with the veil bound across his breast, he threw himself into the waves.

For two nights and two days he was tossed about on the waters. When on the third day the dawn came and the winds fell he saw land very near. He swam eagerly toward it. But when he drew nearer he heard the crash of waves as they struck against rocks that were all covered with foam. Then indeed was Odysseus afraid.

A great wave took hold of him and flung him toward the shore. Now would his bones have been broken upon the rocks if he had not been ready-minded enough to rush toward a rock and to cling to it with both hands until the wave dashed by. Its backward drag took him and carried him back to the deep with the skin stripped from his hands. The waves closed over him. When he rose again he swam round looking for a place where there might be, not rocks, but some easy opening into the land.

At last he saw the mouth of a river. He swam toward it until he felt its stream flowing through the water of the sea. Then in his heart he prayed to the river. "Hear me, O River," was what he said, "I am come to thee as a suppliant, fleeing from the anger of Poseidon, god of the sea. Even by the gods is the man pitied who comes to them as a wanderer and a hapless man. I am thy suppliant, O River; pity me and help me in my need."

Now the river water was smooth for his swimming, and he came safely to its mouth. He came to a place where he might land, but with his flesh swollen and streams of salt water gushing from his mouth and nostrils. He lay on the ground without breath or speech, swooning with the terrible weariness that was upon him. But in a while his breath came back to him and his courage rose. He remembered the veil that the Sea-nymph had given him and he loosened it and let it fall back into the flowing river. A wave came and bore it back to Ino who caught it in her hands.

But Odysseus was still fearful, and he said in his heart, "Ah, me! What is to befall me now? Here am I, naked and forlorn, and I know not amongst what people I am come. And what shall I do with myself when night comes on? If I lie by the river in the frost and dew I may perish of the cold. And if I climb up yonder to the woods and seek refuge in the thickets I may become the prey of wild beasts."

He went from the cold of the river up to the woods, and he found two olive trees growing side by side, twining together so that they made a shelter against the winds. He went and lay between them upon a bed of leaves, and with leaves he covered himself over. There in that shelter, and with that warmth he lay, and sleep came on him, and at last he rested from perils and toils.

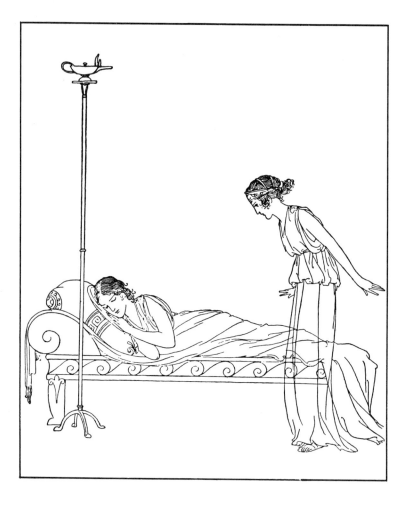

II

AND while he rested the goddess, Pallas Athene, went to the City of the Phæacians, to whose land Odysseus had now come.

She came to the Palace of the King, and, passing through all the doors, came to the chamber where the King's daughter, Nausicaa slept. She entered into Nausicaa's dream, appearing to her in it as one of her girl-comrades. And in the dream she spoke to the Princess:

"Nausicaa," she said, "the garments of your household are all uncared for, and the time is near when, more than ever, you have need to have much and beautiful raiment. Your marriage day will be soon. You will have to have many garments ready by that time — garments to bring with you to your husband's house, and garments to give to those who will attend you at your wedding. There is much to be done, Nausicaa. Be ready at the break of day, and take your maidens with you, and bring the garments of your household to the river to be washed. I will be your mate in the toil. Beg your father to give you a wagon with mules to carry all the garments that we have need to wash."

So in her dream Pallas Athene spoke to the Princess in the likeness of her girl-friend. Having put the task of washing into her mind, the goddess left the Palace of the King and the country of the Phæacians.

Nausicaa, when she rose, thought upon her dream, and she went through the Palace and found her father. He was going to the assembly of the Phæacians. She came to him, but she was shy about speaking of that which had been in her dream — her marriage day — since her parents had not spoken to her about such a thing. Saying that she was going to the river to wash the garments of the household, she asked for a wagon and for mules. "So many garments have I lying soiled," she said. "Yea, and thou too, my father, should have fresh raiment when you go forth to the assembly of the Phæacians. And in our house are the two unwedded youths, my brothers, who are always eager for new washed garments wherein to go to dances."

Her father smiled on her and said, "The mules and wagon thou mayst have, Nausicaa, and the servants shall get them ready for thee now."

He called to the servants and bade them get ready the mules and the wagon. Then Nausicaa gathered her maids together and they brought the soiled garments of the household to the wagon. And her mother, so that Nausicaa and her maids might eat while they were from home, put in a basket filled with dainties and a skin of wine. Also she gave them a jar of olive oil so that they might rub themselves with oil when bathing in the river.

Young Nausicaa herself drove the wagon. She mounted it and took the whip in her hands and started the mules, and they went through fields and by farms and came to the riverbank.

The girls brought the garments to the stream, and leaving them in the shallow parts trod them with their bare feet. The wagon was unharnessed and the mules were left to graze along the riverside. Now when they had washed the garments they took them to the seashore and left them on the clean pebbles to dry in the sun. Then Nausicaa and her companions went into the river and bathed and sported in the water.

When they had bathed they sat down and ate the meal that had been put on the wagon for them. The garments were not yet dried and Nausicaa called on her companions to play. Straightway they took a ball and threw it from one to the other, each singing a song that went with the game. And as they played on the meadow they made a lovely company, and the Princess Nausicaa was the tallest and fairest and noblest of them all.

Before they left the riverside to load the wagon they played a last game. The Princess threw the ball, and the girl whose turn it was to catch missed it. The ball went into the river and was carried down the stream. At that they all raised a cry. It was this cry that woke up Odysseus who, covered over with leaves, was then sleeping in the shelter of the two olive trees.

He crept out from under the thicket, covering his nakedness with leafy boughs that he broke off the trees. And when he saw the girls in the meadow he wanted to go to them to beg for their help. But when they looked on him they were terribly frightened and they ran this way and that way and hid themselves. Only Nausicaa stood still, for Pallas Athene had taken fear from her mind.

Odysseus stood a little way from her and spoke to her in a beseeching voice. "I supplicate thee, lady, to help me in my bitter need. I would kneel to thee and clasp thy knees only I fear thine anger. Have pity upon me. Yesterday was the twentieth day that I was upon the sea, driven hither and thither by the waves and the winds."

And still Nausicaa stood, and Odysseus looking upon her was filled with reverence for her, so noble she seemed. "I know not as I look upon thee," he said, "whether thou art a goddess or a mortal maiden. If thou art a mortal maiden, happy must thy father be and thy mother and thy brothers. Surely they must be proud and glad to see thee in the dance, for thou art the very flower of maidens. And happy above all will he be who will lead thee to his home as his bride. Never have my eyes beheld one who had such beauty and such nobleness. I think thou art like to the young palm tree I once saw springing up by the altar of Apollo in Delos — a tree that many marvelled to look at. O lady, after many and sore trials, to thee, first of all the people, have I come. I know that thou wilt be gracious to me. Show me the way to the town. Give me an old garment to cast about me. And may the gods grant thee thy wish and heart's desire — a noble husband who will cherish thee."

She spoke to him as a Princess should, seeing that in spite of the evil plight he was in, he was a man of worth. "Stranger," she said, "since thou hast come to our land, thou shalt not lack for raiment nor aught else that is given to a suppliant. I will show thee the way to the town also."

He asked what land he was in. "This, stranger," she said, "is the land of the Phæacians, and Alcinous is King over them. And I am the King's daughter, Nausicaa."

Then she called to her companions. "Do not hide yourselves," she said. "This is not an enemy, but a helpless and an unfriended man. We must befriend him, for it is well said that the stranger and the beggar are from God."

The girls came back and they brought Odysseus to a sheltered place and they made him sit down and laid a garment beside him. One brought the jar of olive oil that he might clean himself when he bathed in the river. And Odysseus was very glad to get this oil for his back and shoulders were all crusted over with flakes of brine. He went into the river and bathed and rubbed himself with the oil. Then he put on the garment that had been brought him. So well he looked that when he came toward them again the Princess said to the maids:

"Look now on the man who a while ago seemed so terrifying! He is most handsome and stately. Would that we might see more of him. Now, my maidens, bring the stranger meat and drink."

They came to him and they served him with meat and drink and he ate and drank eagerly, for it was long since he had tasted food. And while he ate, Nausicaa and her companions went down to the seashore and gathered the garments that were now dried, singing songs the while. They harnessed the mules and folded the garments and left them on the wagon.

When they were ready to go Nausicaa went to Odysseus

and said to him, "Stranger, if thou wouldst make thy way into the city come with us now, so that we may guide thee. But first listen to what I would say. While we are going through the fields and by the farms walk thou behind, keeping near the wagon. But when we enter the ways of the City, go no further with us. People might speak unkindly of me if they saw me with a stranger such as thou. They might say, 'Who does Nausicaa bring to her father's house? Someone she would like to make her husband, most likely.' So that we may not meet with such rudeness I would have thee come alone to my father's house. Listen now and I will tell how thou mayst do this."

"There is a grove kept for the goddess Pallas Athene within a man's shout of the city. In that grove is a spring, and when we come near I would have thee go and rest thyself by it. Then when thou dost think we have come to my father's house, enter the City and ask thy way to the palace of the King. When thou hast come to it, pass quickly through the court and through the great chamber and come to where my mother sits weaving yarn by the light of the fire. My father will be sitting near, drinking his wine in the evening. Pass by his seat and come to my mother, and clasp your hands about her knees and ask for her aid. If she becomes friendly to thee thou wilt be helped by our people and wilt be given the means of returning to thine own land."

So Nausicaa bade him. Then she touched the mules with the whip and the wagon went on. Odysseus walked with the maids behind. As the sun set they came to the

grove that was outside the City — the grove of Pallas
Athene. Odysseus went into it and sat by the spring. And
while he was in her grove he prayed to the goddess, "Hear
me, Pallas Athene, and grant that I may come before the
King of this land as one well worthy of his pity and his
help."

III

ABOUT the time that the maiden Nausicaa had come to her father's house, Odysseus rose up from where he sat by the spring in the grove
of Pallas Athene and went into the City. There he met
one who showed him the way to the palace of King Alcinous. The doors of that palace were golden and the doorposts were of silver. And there was a garden by the great
door filled with fruitful trees — pear trees and pomegran-
ates; apple trees and trees bearing figs and olives. Below it
was a vineyard showing clusters of grapes. That orchard
and that vineyard were marvels, for in them never fruit
fell or was gathered but other fruit ripened to take its
place; from season to season there was fruit for the gathering in the king's close.

Odysseus stood before the threshold of bronze and
many thoughts were in his mind. But at last with a prayer
to Zeus he crossed the threshold and went through the
great hall. Now on that evening the Captains and the

Councillors of the Phæacians sat drinking wine with the King. Odysseus passed by them, and stayed not at the King's chair, but went where Arete, the Queen, sat. And he knelt before her and clasped her knees with his hands and spoke to her in supplication:

"Arete, Queen! After many toils and perils I am come to thee and to thy husband, and to these, thy guests! May the gods give all who are here a happy life and may each see his children in safe possession of his halls. I have come to thee to beg that thou wouldst put me on my way to my own land, for long have I suffered sore affliction far from my friends."

Then, having spoken, Odysseus went and sat down in the ashes of the hearth with his head bowed. No one spoke for long. Then an aged Councillor who was there spoke to the King.

"O Alcinous," he said, "it is not right that a stranger should sit in the ashes by thy hearth. Bid the stranger rise now and let a chair be given him and supper set before him."

Then Alcinous took Odysseus by the hand, and raised him from where he sat, and bade his son Laodamas give place to him. He sat on a chair inlaid with silver and the housedame brought him bread and wine and dainties. He ate, and King Alcinous spoke to the company and said:

"Tomorrow I shall call you together and we will entertain this stranger with a feast in our halls, and we shall take counsel to see in what way we can convoy him to his own land."

The Captains and Councillors assented to this, and then each one arose and went to his own house. Odysseus was left alone in the hall with the King and the Queen. Now Arete, looking closely at Odysseus, recognized the mantle he wore, for she herself had wrought it with her handmaids. And when all the company had gone she spoke to Odysseus and said:

"Stranger, who art thou? Didst thou not speak of coming to us from across the deep? And if thou didst come that way, who gave thee the raiment that thou hast on?"

Said Odysseus, "Lady, for seven and ten days I sailed across the deep, and on the eighteenth day I sighted the hills of thy land. But my woes were not yet ended. The storm winds shattered my raft, and when I strove to land the waves overwhelmed me and dashed me against great rocks in a desolate place. At length I came to a river, and I swam through its mouth and I found a shelter from the wind. There I lay amongst the leaves all the night long and from dawn to midday. Then came thy daughter down to the river. I was aware of her playing with her friends, and to her I made my supplication. She gave me bread and wine, and she bestowed these garments upon me, and she showed an understanding that was far beyond her years."

Then said Alcinous the King, "Our daughter did not do well when she did not bring thee straight to our house."

Odysseus said, "My lord, do not blame the maiden. She bade me follow with her company, and she was only care-

ful that no one should have cause to make ill-judged re-
marks upon the stranger whom she found."

Then Alcinous, the King, praised Odysseus and said
that he should like such a man to abide in his house and
that he would give him land and wealth, in the country of
the Phæacians. "But if it is not thy will to abide with us,"
he said, "I shall give thee a ship and a company of men to
take thee to thy own land, even if that land be as far as
Eubœa, which, our men say, is the farthest of all lands."
As he said this Odysseus uttered a prayer in his heart, "O
Father Zeus, grant that Alcinous the King may fulfil all
that he has promised — and for that may his fame never
be quenched — and that I may come to my own land."

Arete now bade the maids prepare a bed for Odysseus.
This they did, casting warm coverlets and purple blankets
upon it. And when Odysseus came to the bed and lay in
it, after the tossing of the waves, rest in it seemed wonderfully good.

At dawn of day he went with the King to the assembly
of the Phæacians. When the Princes and Captains and
Councillors were gathered together, Alcinous spoke to
them saying:

"Princes and Captains and Councillors of the Phæacians! This stranger has come to my house in his wanderings, and he desires us to give him a ship and a company
of men, so that he may cross the sea and come to his own
land. Let us, as in times past we have done for others, help
him in his journey. Nay, let us even now draw down a
black ship to the sea, and put two and fifty of our noblest

youths upon it, and let us make it ready for the voyage. But before he departs from amongst us, come all of you to a feast that I shall give to this stranger in my house. And moreover, let us take with us the minstrel of our land, blind Demodocus, that his songs may make us glad at the feast."

So the King spoke, and the Princes, Captains, and Councillors of the Phæacians went with him to the palace. And at the same time two and fifty youths went down to the shore of the sea, and drew down a ship and placed the masts and sails upon it, and left the oars in their leathern loops. Having done all this they went to the palace where the feast was being given and where many men had gathered.

The henchman led in the minstrel, blind Demodocus. To him the gods had given a good and an evil fortune — the gift of song with the lack of sight. The henchman led him through the company, and placed him on a seat inlaid with silver, and hung his lyre on the pillar above his seat. When the guests and the minstrel had feasted, blind Demodocus took down the lyre and sang of things that were already famous — of the deeds of Achilles and Odysseus.

Now when he heard the words that the minstrel uttered, Odysseus caught up his purple cloak and drew it over his head. Tears were falling down his cheeks and he was ashamed of their being seen. No one marked his weeping except the King, and the King wondered why his guest should be so moved by what the minstrel related.

When they had feasted and the minstrel had sung to them, Alcinous said, "Let us go forth now and engage in games and sports so that our stranger guest may tell his friends when he is amongst them what our young men can do."

All went out from the palace to the place where the games were played. There was a foot race, and there was a boxing match, and there was wrestling and weight throwing. All the youths present went into the games. And when the sports were ending Laodamas, the son of King Alcinous, said to his friends:

"Come, my friends, and let us ask the stranger whether he is skilled or practised in any sport." And saying this he went to Odysseus and said, "Friend and stranger, come now and try thy skill in the games. Cast care away from thee, for thy journey shall not be long delayed. Even now the ship is drawn down to the sea, and we have with us the company of youths that is ready to help thee to thine own land."

Said Odysseus, "Sorrow is nearer to my heart than sport, for much have I endured in times that are not far past."

Then a youth who was with Laodamas, Euryalus, who had won in the wrestling bout, said insolently, "Laodamas is surely mistaken in thinking that thou shouldst be proficient in sports. As I look at thee I think that thou art one who makes voyages for gain — a trader whose only thought is for his cargo and his gains."

Then said Odysseus with anger. "Thou hast not spoken well, young man. Thou hast beauty surely, but thou hast

not grace of manner nor speech. And thou hast stirred the spirit in my breast by speaking to me in such words."

Thereupon, clad as he was in his mantle, Odysseus sprang up and took a weight that was larger than any yet lifted, and with one whirl he flung it from his hands. Beyond all marks it flew, and one who was standing far off cried out, "Even a blind man, stranger, might know that thy weight need not be confused with the others, but lies far beyond them. In this bout none of the Phæacians can surpass thee."

And Odysseus, turning to the youths, said, "Let who will, pass that throw. And if any of you would try with me in boxing or wrestling or even in the foot race, let him stand forward — anyone except Laodamas, for he is of the house that has befriended me. A rude man he would surely be who should strive with his host."

All kept silence. Then Alcinous the King said, "So that thou shalt have something to tell thy friends when thou art in thine own land, we shall show thee the games in which we are most skilful. For we Phæacians are not perfect boxers or wrestlers, but we excell all in running and in dancing and in pulling with the oar. Lo, now, ye dancers! Come forward and show your nimbleness, so that the stranger may tell his friends, when he is amongst them, how far we surpass all men in dancing as well as in seamanship and speed of foot."

A place was levelled for the dance, and the blind minstrel, Demodocus, took the lyre in his hands and made music, while youths skilled in the dance struck the ground with their feet. Odysseus as he watched them marvelled at their grace and their spirit. When the dance was ended he said to the King, "My Lord Alcinous, thou didst boast thy dancers to be the best in the world, and thy word is not to be denied. I wonder as I look upon them."

At the end of the day Alcinous spoke to his people and said, "This stranger, in all that he does and says, shows himself to be a wise and a mighty man. Let each of us now give him the stranger's gift. Here there are twelve princes of the Phæacians and I am the thirteenth. Let each of us give him a worthy gift, and then let us go back to my house and sit down to supper. As for Euryalus, let him make amends to the stranger for his rudeness of speech as he offers him his gift."

All assented to the King's words, and Euryalus went to Odysseus and said, "Stranger, if I have spoken aught that offended thee, may the storm winds snatch it and bear it away. May the gods grant that thou shalt see thy wife and come to thine own country. Too long hast thou endured afflictions away from thy friends."

So saying, Euryalus gave Odysseus a sword of bronze with a silver hilt and a sheath of ivory. Odysseus took it and said, "And to you, my friend, may the gods grant all happiness, and mayst thou never miss the sword that thou hast given me. Thy gracious speech hath made full amends."

Each of the twelve princes gave gifts to Odysseus, and the gifts were brought to the palace and left by the side of the Queen. And Arete herself gave Odysseus a beautiful

coffer with raiment and gold in it, and Alcinous, the King, gave him a beautiful cup, all of gold.

In the palace the bath was prepared for Odysseus, and he entered it and was glad of the warm water, for not since he had left the Island of Calypso did he have a warm bath. He came from the bath and put on the beautiful raiment that had been given him and he walked through the hall, looking for a king amongst men.

Now the maiden, Nausicaa, stood by a pillar as he passed, and she knew that she had never looked upon a man who was more splendid. She had thought that the stranger whom she had saved would have stayed in her father's house, and that one day he would be her husband. But now she knew that by no means would he abide in the land of the Phæacians. As he passed by, she spoke to him and said, "Farewell, O Stranger! And when thou art in thine own country, think sometimes of me, Nausicaa, who helped thee." Odysseus took her hand and said to her, "Farewell, daughter of King Alcinous! May Zeus grant that I may return to my own land. There every day shall I pay homage to my memory of thee, to whom I owe my life."

He passed on and he came to where the Princes and Captains and Councillors of the Phæacians sat. His seat was beside the King's. Then the henchman brought in the minstrel, blind Demodocus, and placed him on a seat by a pillar. And when supper was served Odysseus sent to Demodocus a portion of his own meat. He spoke too in praise of the minstrel saying, "Right well dost thou sing of the Greeks and all they wrought and suffered — as well, methinks, as if thou hadst been present at the war of Troy. I would ask if thou canst sing of the Wooden Horse that brought destruction to the Trojans. If thou canst, I shall be a witness amongst all men how the gods have surely given thee the gift of song."

Demodocus took down the lyre and sang. His song told how one part of the Greek sailed away in their ships and how others with Odysseus to lead them were now in the center of Priam's City all hidden in the great Wooden Horse which the Trojans themselves had dragged across their broken wall. So the Wooden Horse stood, and the people gathered around talked of what should be done with so wonderful a thing — whether to break open its timbers, or drag it to a steep hill and hurl it down on the rocks, or leave it there as an offering to the gods. As an offering to the gods it was left at last. Then the minstrel sang how Odysseus and his comrades poured forth from the hollow of the horse and took the City.

As the minstrel sang, the heart of Odysseus melted within him and tears fell down his cheeks. None of the company saw him weeping except Alcinous the King. But the King cried out to the company saying, "Let the minstrel cease, for there is one amongst us to whom his song is not pleasing. Ever since it began the stranger here has wept with tears flowing down his cheeks."

The minstrel ceased, and all the company looked in surprise at Odysseus, who sat with his head bowed and his mantle wrapped around his head. Why did he weep? each man asked. No one had asked of him his name, for each thought it was more noble to serve a stranger without knowing his name.

Said the King, speaking again, "In a brother's place stands the stranger and the suppliant, and as a brother art thou to us, O unknown guest. But wilt thou not be brotherly to us? Tell us by what name they call thee in thine own land. Tell us, too, of thy land and thy city. And tell us, too, where thou wert borne on thy wanderings, and to what lands and peoples thou camest. And as a brother tell us why thou dost weep and mourn in spirit over the tale of the going forth of the Greeks to the war of Troy. Didst thou have a kinsman who fell before Priam's City — a daughter's husband, or a wife's father, or someone nearer by blood? Or didst thou have a loving friend who fell there — one with an understanding heart who wast to thee as a brother?"

Such questions the King asked, and Odysseus taking the mantle from around his head turned round to the company.

IV

THEN Odysseus spoke before the company and said, "O Alcinous, famous King, it is good to listen to a minstrel such as Demodocus is. And as for me, I know of no greater delight than when men feast together with open hearts, when tables are plentifully spread, when wine-bearers pour out good wine into cups, and when a minstrel sings to them noble songs. This seems to me to be happiness indeed. But thou hast asked me to speak of my wanderings and my toils. Ah, where can I begin that tale? For the gods have given me more woes than a man can speak of!

"But first of all I will declare to you my name and my country. I am Odysseus, son of Laertes, and my land is Ithaka, an island around which many islands lie. Ithaka is a rugged isle, but a good nurse of hardy men, and I, for one, have found that there is no place fairer than a man's own land. But now I will tell thee, King, and tell the Princes and Captains and Councillors of the Phæacians, the tale of my wanderings.

"The wind bore my ships from the coast of Troy, and with our white sails hoisted we came to the cape that is called Malea. Now if we had been able to double this cape we should soon have come to our own country, all unhurt. But the north wind came and swept us from our course and drove us wandering past Cythera.

"Then for nine days we were borne onward by terrible winds, and away from all known lands. On the tenth day we came to a strange country. Many of my men landed there. The people of that land were harmless and friendly, but the land itself was most dangerous. For there grew there the honey-sweet fruit of the lotus that makes all men forgetful of their past and neglectful of their future. And those of my men who ate the lotus that the dwellers of that land offered them became forgetful of their country and of the way before them. They wanted to abide forever in the land of the lotus. They wept when they thought of all the toils before them and of all they had endured. I led them back to the ships, and I had to place them beneath the benches and leave them in bonds. And I commanded those who had ate of the lotus to go at once aboard the ships. Then, when I had got all my men upon the ships, we made haste to sail away.

"Later we came to the land of the Cyclôpes, a giant people. There is a waste island outside the harbor of their land, and on it there is a well of bright water that has poplars growing round it. We came to that empty island, and we beached our ships and took down our sails.

"As soon as the dawn came we went through the empty island, starting the wild goats that were there in flocks, and shooting them with our arrows. We killed so many wild goats there that we had nine for each ship. Afterwards we looked across to the land of the Cyclôpes, and we heard the sound of voices and saw the smoke of fires and heard the bleating of flocks of sheep and goats.

"I called my companions together and I said, 'It would be well for some of us to go to that other island. With my own ship and with the company that is on it I shall go there. The rest of you abide here. I will find out what manner of men live there, and whether they will treat us kindly and give us gifts that are due to strangers — gifts of provisions for our voyage.'

"We embarked and we came to the land. There was a

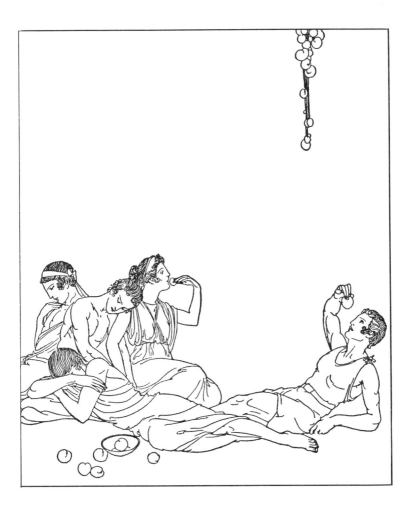

cave near the sea, and round the cave there were mighty flocks of sheep and goats. I took twelve men with me and I left the rest to guard the ship. We went into the cave and found no man there. There were baskets filled with cheeses, and vessels of whey, and pails and bowls of milk. My men wanted me to take some of the cheeses and drive off some of the lambs and kids and come away. But this I would not do, for I would rather that he who owned the stores would give us of his own free will the offerings that were due to strangers.

"While we were in the cave, he whose dwelling it was, returned to it. He carried on his shoulder a great pile of wood for his fire. Never in our lives did we see a creature so frightful as this Cyclops was. He was a giant in size, and, what made him terrible to behold, he had but one eye, and that single eye was in his forehead. He cast down on the ground the pile of wood that he carried, making such a din that we fled in terror into the corners and recesses of the cave. Next he drove his flocks into the cave and began to milk his ewes and goats. And when he had the flocks within, he took up a stone that not all our strengths could move and set it as a door to the mouth of the cave.

"The Cyclops kindled his fire, and when it blazed up he saw us in the corners and recesses. He spoke to us. We knew not what he said, but our hearts were shaken with terror at the sound of his deep voice.

"I spoke to him saying that we were Agamemnon's men on our way home from the taking of Priam's City, and I begged him to deal with us kindly, for the sake of Zeus who is ever in the company of strangers and suppliants. But he answered me saying, 'We Cyclôpes pay no heed to Zeus, nor to any of thy gods. In our strength and our power we deem that we are mightier than they. I will not spare thee, neither will I give thee aught for the sake of Zeus, but only as my own spirit bids me. And first I would have thee tell me how you came to our land.'

"I knew it would be better not to let the Cyclops know that my ship and my companions were at the harbor of the island. Therefore I spoke to him guilefully, telling him that my ship had been broken on the rocks, and that I and the men with me were the only ones who had escaped utter doom.

"I begged again that he would deal with us as just men deal with strangers and suppliants, but he, without saying a word, laid hands upon two of my men, and swinging them by the legs, dashed their brains out on the earth. He cut them to pieces and ate them before our very eyes. We wept and we prayed to Zeus as we witnessed a deed so terrible.

"Next the Cyclops stretched himself amongst his sheep and went to sleep beside the fire. Then I debated whether I should take my sharp sword in my hand, and feeling where his heart was, stab him there. But second thoughts held me back from doing this. I might be able to kill him as he slept, but not even with my companions could I roll away the great stone that closed the mouth of the cave.

"Dawn came, and the Cyclops awakened, kindled his

fire and milked his flocks. Then he seized two others of my men and made ready for his midday meal. And now he rolled away the great stone and drove his flocks out of the cave.

"I had pondered on a way of escape, and I had thought of something that might be done to baffle the Cyclops. I had with me a great skin of sweet wine, and I thought that if I could make him drunken with wine I and my companions might be able for him. But there were other preparations to be made first. On the floor of the cave there was a great beam of olive wood which the Cyclops had cut to make a club when the wood should be seasoned. It was yet green. I and my companions went and cut off a fathom's length of the wood, and sharpened it to a point and took it to the fire and hardened it in the glow. Then I hid the beam in a recess of the cave.

"The Cyclops came back in the evening, and opening up the cave drove in his flocks. Then he closed the cave again with the stone and went and milked his ewes and his goats. Again he seized two of my companions. I went to the terrible creature with a bowl of wine in my hands. He took it and drank it and cried out, 'Give me another bowl of this, and tell me thy name that I may give thee gifts for bringing me this honey-tasting drink.'

"Again I spoke to him guilefully and said, 'Noman is my name. Noman my father and my mother call me.' "

" 'Give me more of the drink, Noman,' he shouted. 'And the gift that I shall give to thee is that I shall make thee the last of thy fellows to be eaten.'

"I gave him wine again, and when he had taken the third bowl he sank backwards with his face upturned, and sleep came upon him. Then I, with four companions, took that beam of olive wood, now made into a hard and pointed stake, and thrust it into the ashes of the fire. When the pointed end began to glow we drew it out of the flame. Then I and my companions laid hold on the great stake and, dashing at the Cyclops, thrust it into his eye. He raised a terrible cry that made the rocks ring and we dashed away into the recesses of the cave.

"His cries brought other Cyclôpes to the mouth of the cave, and they, naming him as Polyphemus, called out and asked him what ailed him to cry. 'Noman,' he shrieked out, 'Noman is slaying me by guile.' They answered him saying, 'If no man is slaying thee, there is nothing we can do for thee, Polyphemus. What ails thee has been sent to thee by the gods.' Saying this, they went away from the mouth of the cave without attempting to move away the stone.

"Polyphemus then, groaning with pain, rolled away the stone and sat before the mouth of the cave with his hands outstretched, thinking that he would catch us as we dashed out. I showed my companions how we might pass by him. I laid hands on certain rams of the flock and I lashed three of them together with supple rods. Then on the middle ram I put a man of my company. Thus every three rams carried a man. As soon as the dawn had come the rams hastened out to the pasture, and, as they passed, Polyphemus laid hands on the first and the third of each three that went by. They passed out and Polyphemus did not guess that a ram that he did not touch carried out a man.

"For myself, I took a ram that was the strongest and fleeciest of the whole flock and I placed myself under him, clinging to the wool of his belly. As this ram, the best of all his flock, went by, Polyphemus, laying his hands upon him, said, 'Would that you, the best of my flock, were endowed with speech, so that you might tell me where Noman, who has blinded me, has hidden himself.' The ram went by him, and when he had gone a little way from the cave I loosed myself from him and went and set my companions free.

"We gathered together many of Polyphemus' sheep and we drove them down to our ship. The men we had left behind would have wept when they heard what had happened to six of their companions. But I bade them take on board the sheep we had brought and pull the ship away from that land. Then when he had drawn a certain distance from the shore I could not forbear to shout my taunts into the cave of Polyphemus. 'Cyclops,' I cried, 'you thought that you had the company of a fool and a weakling to eat. But you have been worsted by me, and your evil deeds have been punished.'

"So I shouted, and Polyphemus came to the mouth of the cave with great anger in his heart. He took up rocks and cast them at the ship and they fell before the prow. The men bent to the oars and pulled the ship away or it would have been broken by the rocks he cast. And when we were further away I shouted to him:

" 'Cyclops, if any man should ask who it was set his mark upon you, say that he was Odysseus, the son of Laertes.'

"Then I heard Polyphemus cry out, 'I call upon Poseidon, the god of the sea, whose son I am, to avenge me upon you, Odysseus. I call upon Poseidon to grant that you, Odysseus, may never come to your home, or if the gods have ordained your return, that you come to it after much toil and suffering, in an evil plight and in a stranger's ship, to find sorrow in your home.'

"So Polyphemus prayed, and, to my evil fortune, Poseidon heard his prayer. But we went on in our ship rejoicing at our escape. We came to the waste island where my other ships were. All the company rejoiced to see us, although they had to mourn for their six companions slain by Polyphemus. We divided amongst the ships the sheep we had taken from Polyphemus' flock and we sacrificed to the gods. At the dawn of the next day we raised the sails on each ship and we sailed away."

V

WE came to the Island where Æolus, the Lord of the Winds, he who can give mariners a good or a bad wind, has his dwelling. With his six sons and his six daughters Æolus lives on a floating island that has all around it a wall of bronze. And when we came to his island, the Lord of the Winds treated us kindly and kept us at his dwelling for a month. Now when the time came for us to leave, Æolus did not try to hold us on the island. And to me, when I was going down to the ships, he gave a bag made from the hide of an ox, and in that bag were all the winds that blow. He made the mouth of the bag fast with a silver thong, so that no wind that might drive us from our course would escape. Then he sent the West Wind to blow on our sails that we might reach our own land as quickly as a ship might go.

"For nine days we sailed with the West Wind driving us, and on the tenth day we came in sight of Ithaka, our own land. We saws its coast and the beacon fires upon the coast and the people tending the fires. Then I thought that the curse of the Cyclops was vain and could bring no harm to us. Sleep that I had kept from me for long I let weigh me down, and I no longer kept watch.

"Then even as I slept, the misfortune that I had watched against fell upon me. For now my men spoke together and said, 'There is our native land, and we come back to it after ten years' struggles and toils, with empty hands. Different it is with our lord, Odysseus. He brings gold and silver from Priam's treasure chamber in Troy. And Æolus too has given him a treasure in an oxhide bag. But let us take something out of that bag while he sleeps.

"So they spoke, and they unloosed the mouth of the bag, and behold! All the winds that were tied in it burst out. Then the winds drove our ship toward the high seas and away from our land. What became of the other ships

I know not. I awoke and I found that we were being driven here and there by the winds. I did not know whether I should spring into the sea and so end all my troubles, or whether I should endure this terrible misfortune. I muffled my head in my cloak and lay on the deck of my ship.

"The winds brought us back again to the floating Island. We landed and I went to the dwelling of the Lord of the Winds. I sat by the pillars of his threshold and he came out and spoke to me. 'How now, Odysseus?' said he. 'How is it thou hast returned so soon? Did I not give thee a fair wind to take thee to thine own country, and did I not tie up all the winds that might be contrary to thee?'

" 'My evil companions,' I said, 'have been my bane. They have undone all the good that thou didst for me, O King of the Winds. They opened the bag and let all the winds fly out. And now help me, O Lord Æolus, once again.'

"But Æolus said to me, 'Far be it from me to help such a man as thou — a man surely accursed by the gods. Go from my Island, for nothing will I do for thee.' Then I went from his dwelling and took my way down to the ship.

"We sailed away from the Island of Æolus with heavy hearts. Next we came to the Æean Island, where we met with Circe, the Enchantress. For two days and two nights we were on that island without seeing the sign of a habitation. On the third day I saw smoke rising up from some hearth. I spoke of it to my men, and it seemed good to us that part of our company should go to see were there people there who might help us. We drew lots to find out who should go, and it fell to the lot of Eurylochus to go with part of the company, while I remained with the other part.

"So Eurylochus went with two and twenty men. In the forest glades they came upon a house built of polished stones. All round that house wild beasts roamed — wolves and lions. But these beasts were not fierce. As Eurylochus and his men went toward the house the lions and wolves fawned upon them like house dogs.

"But the men were affrighted and stood round the outer gate of the court. They heard a voice within the house singing, and it seemed to them to be the voice of a woman, singing as she went to and fro before a web she was weaving on a loom. The men shouted, and she who had been singing opened the polished doors and came out of the dwelling. She was very fair to see. As she opened the doors of the house she asked the men to come within and they went into her halls.

"But Eurylochus tarried behind. He watched the woman and he saw her give food to the men. But he saw that she mixed a drug with what she gave them to eat and with the wine she gave them to drink. No sooner had they eaten the food and drunk the wine than she struck them with a wand, and behold! The men turned into swine. Then the woman drove them out of the house and put them in the swinepens and gave them acorns and mast and the fruit of the cornel tree to eat.

"Eurylochus, when he saw these happenings, ran back

through the forest and told me all. Then I cast about my shoulder my good sword of bronze, and, bidding Eurylochus stay by the ships, I went through the forest and came to the house of the enchantress. I stood at the outer court and called out. Then Circe the Enchantress flung wide the shining doors, and called to me to come within. I entered her dwelling and she brought me to a chair and put a footstool under my feet. Then she brought me in a golden cup the wine into which she had cast a harmful drug.

"As she handed me the cup I drew my sword and sprang at her as one eager to slay her. She shrank back from me and cried out, 'Who art thou who art able to guess at my enchantments? Verily, thou art Odysseus, of whom Hermes told me. Nay, put up thy sword and let us two be friendly to each other. In all things I will treat thee kindly.'

"But I said to her, 'Nay, Circe, you must swear to me first that thou wilt not treat me guilefully.'

"She swore by the gods that she would not treat me guilefully, and I put up my sword. Then the handmaidens of Circe prepared a bath, and I bathed and rubbed myself with olive oil, and Circe gave me a new mantle and doublet. The handmaidens brought out silver tables, and on them set golden baskets with bread and meat in them, and others brought cups of honey-tasting wine. I sat before a silver table but I had no pleasure in the food before me.

"When Circe saw me sitting silent and troubled she said, 'Why, Odysseus, dost thou sit like a speechless man?

Dost thou think there is a drug in this food? But I have sworn that I will not treat thee guilefully, and that oath I shall keep.'

"And I said to her, 'O Circe, Enchantress, what man of good heart could take meat and drink while his companions are as swine in swinepens? If thou wouldst have me eat and drink, first let me see my companions in their own forms.'

"Circe, when she heard me say this, went to the swinepen and anointed each of the swine that was there with a charm. As she did, the bristles dropped away and the limbs of the man were seen. My companions became men again, and were even taller and handsomer than they had been before.

"After that we lived on Circe's island in friendship with the enchantress. She did not treat us guilefully again and we feasted in her house for a year.

"But in all of us there was a longing to return to our own land. And my men came to me and craved that I should ask Circe to let us go on our homeward way. She gave us leave to go and she told us of the many dangers we should meet on our voyage."

VI

WHEN the sun sank and darkness came on, my men went to lie by the hawsers of the ship. Then Circe the Enchantress took my hand, and, making me sit down by her, told me of the voyage that was before us.

" 'To the Sirens first you shall come,' said she, 'to the Sirens, who sit in their field of flowers and bewitch all men who come near them. He who comes near the Sirens without knowing their ways and hears the sound of their voices — never again shall that man see wife or child, or have joy of his home-coming. All round where the Sirens sit are great heaps of the bones of men. But I will tell thee, Odysseus, how thou mayst pass them.'

" 'When thou comest near put wax over the ears of thy company lest any of them hear the Sirens' song. But if thou thyself art minded to hear, let thy company bind thee hand and foot to the mast. And if thou shalt beseech them to loose thee, then must they bind thee with tighter bonds. When thy companions have driven the ship past where the Sirens sing then thou canst be unbound.'

" 'Past where the Sirens sit there is a dangerous place indeed. On one side there are great rocks which the gods call the Rocks Wandering. No ship ever escapes that goes that way. And round these rocks the planks of ships and the bodies of men are tossed by waves of the sea and storms of fire. One ship only ever passed that way, Jason's ship, the *Argo*, and that ship would have been broken on the rocks if Hera the goddess had not helped it to pass, because of her love for the hero Jason.'

" 'On the other side of the Rocks Wandering are two peaks through which thou wilt have to take thy ship. One peak is smooth and sheer and goes up to the clouds of heaven. In the middle of it there is a cave, and that cave is the den of a monster named Scylla. This monster has six necks and on each neck there is a hideous head. She holds her heads over the gulf, seeking for prey and yelping horribly. No ship has ever passed that way without Scylla seizing and carrying off in each mouth of her six heads the body of a man.'

" 'The other peak is near. Thou couldst send an arrow across to it from Scylla's den. Out of the peak a fig tree grows, and below that fig tree Charybdis has her den. She sits there sucking down the water and spouting it forth. Mayst thou not be near when she sucks the water down, for then nothing could save thee. Keep nearer to Scylla's than to Charybdis's rock. It is better to lose six of your company than to lose thy ship and all thy company. Keep near Scylla's rock and drive right on.'

" 'If thou shouldst win past the deadly rocks guarded by Scylla and Charybdis thou wilt come to the Island of Thrinacia. There the Cattle of the Sun graze with immortal nymphs to guard them. If thou comest to that Island, do no hurt to those herds. If thou doest hurt to them I forsee ruin for thy ship and thy men, even though thou thyself shouldst escape.'

"So Circe spoke to me, and having told me such things she took her way up the island. Then I went to the ship and roused my men. Speedily they went aboard, and, having taken their seats upon the benches, struck the water with their oars. Then the sails were hoisted and a breeze came and we sailed away from the Isle of Circe, the Enchantress.

"I told my companions what Circe had told me about the Sirens in their field of flowers. I took a great piece of wax and broke it and kneaded it until it was soft. Then I covered the ears of my men, and they bound me upright to the mast of the ship. The wind dropped and the sea became calm as though a god had stilled the waters. My company took their oars and pulled away. When the ship was within a man's shout from the land we had come near the Sirens espied us and raised their song.

" 'Come hither, come hither, O Odysseus,' the Sirens sang, 'stay thy bark and listen to our song. None hath ever gone this way in his ship until he hath heard from our own lips the voice sweet as a honeycomb, and hath joy of it, and gone on his way a wiser man. We know all things — all the travail the Greeks had in the war of Troy, and we know all that hereafter shall be upon the earth. Odysseus, Odysseus, come to our field of flowers, and hear the song that we shall sing to thee.'

"My heart was mad to listen to the Sirens. I nodded my head to the company commanding them to unloose me, but they bound me the tighter, and bent to their oars and rowed on. When we had gone past the place of the Sirens the men took the wax from off their ears and loosed me from the mast.

"But no sooner had we passed the Island than I saw smoke arising and heard the roaring of the sea. My company threw down their oars in terror. I went amongst them to hearten them, and I made them remember how, by my device, we had escaped from the Cave of the Cyclops. I told them nothing of the monster Scylla, lest the fear of her should break their hearts. And now we began to drive through that narrow strait. On one side was Scylla and on the other Charybdis. Fear gripped the men when they saw Charybdis gulping down the sea. But as we drove by, the monster Scylla seized six of my company — the hardiest of the men who were with me. As they were lifted up in the mouths of her six heads they called to me in their agony. But I could do nothing to aid them. They were carried up to be devoured in the monster's den. Of all the sights I have seen on the ways of the water, that sight was the most pitiful.

"Having passed the rocks of Scylla and Charybdis we came to the Island of Thrinacia. While we were yet on the ship I heard the lowing of the Cattle of the Sun. I spoke to my company and told them that we should drive past that Island and not venture to go upon it.

"The hearts of my men were broken within them at that sentence, and Eurylochus answered me, speaking sadly.

" 'It is easy for thee, O Odysseus, to speak like that, for thou art never weary, and thou hast strength beyond

measure. But is thy heart, too, of iron that thou wilt not suffer thy companions to set foot upon shore where they may rest themselves from the sea and prepare their supper at their ease?'

"So Eurylochus spoke and the rest of the company joined in what he said. Their force was greater than mine. Then said I, 'Swear to me a mighty oath, one and all of you, that if we go upon this Island none of you will slay the cattle out of any herd.'

"They swore the oath that I gave them. We brought our ship to a harbor, and landed near a spring of fresh water, and the men got their supper ready. Having eaten their supper they fell to weeping for they thought upon their comrades that Scylla had devoured. Then they slept.

"The dawn came, but we found that we could not take our ship out of the harbor, for the North Wind and the East Wind blew a hurricane. So we stayed upon the Island and the days and the weeks went by. When the corn we had brought in the ship was all eaten the men went through the island fishing and hunting. Little they got to stay their hunger.

"One day while I slept, Eurylochus gave the men a most evil counsel. 'Every death,' he said, 'is hateful to man, but death by hunger is by far the worst. Rather than die of hunger let us drive off the best cattle from the herds of the Sun. Then, if the gods would wreck us on the sea for the deed, let them do it. I would rather perish on the waves than die in the pangs of hunger.'

"So he spoke, and the rest of the men approved of what

he said. They slaughtered them and roasted their flesh. It was then that I awakened from my sleep. As I came down to the ship the smell of the roasting flesh came to me. Then I knew that a terrible deed had been committed and that a dreadful thing would befall all of us.

"For six days my company feasted on the best of the cattle. On the seventh day the winds ceased to blow. Then we went to the ship and set up the mast and the sails and fared out again on the deep.

"But, having left that island, no other land appeared, and only sky and sea were to be seen. A cloud stayed always above our ship and beneath that cloud the sea was darkened. The West Wind came in a rush, and the mast broke, and, in breaking, struck off the head of the pilot, and he fell straight down into the sea. A thunderbolt struck the ship and the men were swept from the deck. Never a man of my company did I see again.

"The West Wind ceased to blow but the South Wind came and it drove the ship back on its course. It rushed toward the terrible rocks of Scylla and Charybdis. All night long I was borne on, and, at the rising of the sun, I found myself near Charybdis. My ship was sucked down. But I caught the branches of the fig tree that grew out of the rock and hung to it like a bat. There I stayed until the timbers of my ship were cast up again by Charybdis. I dropped down on them. Sitting on the boards I rowed with my hands and passed the rock of Scylla without the monster seeing me.

"Then for nine days I was borne along by the waves,

and on the tenth day I came to Ogygia where the nymph Calypso dwells. She took me to her dwelling and treated me kindly. But why tell the remainder of my toils? To thee, O King, and to thy noble wife I told how I came from Calypso's Island, and I am not one to repeat a plain-told tale."

VII

ODYSSEUS finished, and the company in the hall sat silent, like men enchanted. Then King Alcinous spoke and said, "Never, as far as we Phæacians are concerned, wilt thou, Odysseus, be driven from thy homeward way. Tomorrow we will give thee a ship and an escort, and we will land thee in Ithaka, thine own country." The Princes, Captains and Councillors, marvelling that they had met the renowned Odysseus, went each to his own home. When the dawn had come, each carried down to the ship on which Odysseus was to sail, gifts for him.

When the sun was near its setting they all came back to the King's hall to take farewell of him. The King poured out a great bowl of wine as an offering to the gods. Then Odysseus rose up and placed in the Queen's hands a two-handled cup, and he said, "Farewell to thee, O Queen! Mayst thou long rejoice in thy house and thy children, and in thy husband, Alcinous, the renowned King."

He passed over the threshold of the King's house, and he went down to the ship. He went aboard and lay down on the deck on a sheet and rug that had been spread for him. Straightway the mariners took to their oars, and hoisted their sails, and the ship sped on like a strong sea bird. Odysseus slept. And lightly the ship sped on, bearing that man who had suffered so much sorrow of heart in passing through wars of men and through troublous seas — the ship sped on, and he slept, and was forgetful of all he had passed through.

When the dawn came the ship was near to the Island of Ithaka. The mariners drove to a harbor near which there was a great cave. They ran the ship ashore and lifted out Odysseus, wrapped in the sheet and the rugs, and still sleeping. They left him on the sandy shore of his own land. Then they took the gifts which the King and Queen, the Princes, Captains and Councillors of the Phæacians had given him, and they set them by an olive tree, a little apart from the road, so that no wandering person might come upon them before Odysseus had awakened. Then they went back to their ship and departed from Ithaka for their own land.

Odysseus awakened on the beach of his own land. A mist lay over all, and he did not know what land he had come to. He thought that the Phæacians had left him forsaken on a strange shore. As he looked around him in his bewilderment he saw one who was like a King's son approaching.

Now the one who came near him was not a young man,

but the goddess, Pallas Athene, who had made herself look like a young man. Odysseus arose, and questioned her as to the land he had come to. The goddess answered him and said, "This is Ithaka, a land good for goats and cattle, a land of woods and wells."

Even as she spoke she changed from the semblance of a young man and was seen by Odysseus as a woman tall and fair. "Dost thou not know me, Pallas Athene, the daughter of Zeus, who has always helped thee?" the goddess said. "I would have been more often by thy side, only I did not want to go openly against my brother, Poseidon, the god of the sea, whose son, Polyphemus, thou didst blind."

As the goddess spoke the mist that lay on the land scattered and Odysseus saw that he was indeed in Ithaka, his own country — he knew the harbor and the cave, and the hill Neriton all covered with its forest. And knowing them he knelt down on the ground and kissed the earth of his country.

Then the goddess helped him to lay his goods within the cave — the gold and the bronze and the woven raiment that the Phæacians had given him. She made him sit beside her under the olive tree while she told him of the things that were happening in his house.

"There is trouble in thy halls, Odysseus," she said, "and it would be well for thee not to make thyself known for a time. Harden thy heart, that thou mayest endure for a while longer ill treatment at the hands of men." She told him about the wooers of his wife, who filled his halls all day, and wasted his substance, and who would slay him, lest he should punish them for their insolence. "So that the doom of Agamemnon shall not befall thee — thy slaying within thine own halls — I will change thine appearance that no man shall know thee," the goddess said.

Then she made a change in his appearance that would have been evil but that it was to last for a while only. She made his skin wither, and she dimmed his shining eyes. She made his yellow hair gray and scanty. Then she changed his raiment to a beggar's wrap, torn and stained with smoke. Over his shoulder she cast the hide of a deer, and she put into his hands a beggar's staff, with a tattered bag and a cord to hang it by. And when she had made this change in his appearance the goddess left Odysseus and went from Ithaka.

It was then that she came to Telemachus in Sparta and counselled him to leave the house of Menelaus and Helen; and it has been told how he went with Peisistratus, the son of Nestor, and came to his own ship. His ship was hailed by a man who was flying from those who would slay him, and this man Telemachus took aboard. The stranger's name was Theoclymenus, and he was a soothsayer and a second-sighted man.

And Telemachus, returning to Ithaka, was in peril of his life. The wooers of his mother had discovered that he had gone from Ithaka in a ship. Two of the wooers, Antinous and Eurymachus, were greatly angered at the daring act of the youth. "He has gone to Sparta for help," Antinous said, "and if he finds that there are those who will help him we will not be able to stand against his pride. He will make us suffer for what we have wasted in his house. But let us too act. I will take a ship with twenty men, and lie in wait for him in a strait between Ithaka and Samos, and put an end to his search for his father."

Thereupon Antinous took twenty men to a ship, and fixing mast and sails they went over the sea. There is a little isle between Ithaka and Samos — Asteris it is called — and in the harbor of that isle he and his men lay in wait for Telemachus.

VIII

NEAR the place where Odysseus had landed there lived an old man who was a faithful servant in his house. Eumæus was his name, and he was a swineherd. He had made for himself a dwelling in the wildest part of the island, and had built a wall round it, and had made for the swinepens in the courtyard — twelve pens, and in each pen there were fifty swine. Old Eumæus lived in this place tending the swine with three young men to help him. The swinepens were guarded by four dogs that were as fierce as the beasts of the forest.

As he came near the dogs dashed at him, yelping and snapping; and Odysseus might have suffered foul hurt if the swineherd had not run out of the courtyard and driven the fierce dogs away. Seeing before him one who looked an ancient beggar, Eumæus said, "Old man, it is well that my dogs did not tear thee, for they might have brought upon me the shame of thy death. I have grief and pains enough, the gods know, without such a happening. Here I sit, mourning for my noble master, and fattening hogs for others to eat, while he, mayhap, is wandering in hunger through some friendless city. But come in, old man. I have bread and wine to give thee."

The swineherd led the seeming beggar into the courtyard, and he let him sit down on a heap of brushwood, and spread for him a shaggy goatskin. Odysseus was glad of his servant's welcome, and he said, "May Zeus and all the other gods grant thee thy heart's dearest wish for the welcome that thou has given to me."

Said Eumæus the swineherd, "A good man looks on all strangers and beggars as being from Zeus himself. And my heart's dearest wish is that my master Odysseus should return. Ah, if Odysseus were here, he would give me something which I could hold as mine own — a piece of ground to till, and a wife to comfort me. But my master will not return, and we thralls must go in fear when young lords come to rule it over them."

He went to the swinepens and brought out two sucking pigs; he slaughtered them and cut them small and roasted the meat. When all was cooked, he brought portions to Odysseus sprinkled with barley meal, and he brought him, too, wine in a deep bowl of ivy wood. And when Odysseus had eaten and drunken, Eumæus the swineherd said to him:

"Old man, no wanderer ever comes to this land but that

our lady Penelope sends for him, and gives him entertainment, hoping that he will have something to tell her of her lord, Odysseus. They all do as thou wouldst do if thou camest to her — tell her a tale of having seen or of having heard of her lord, to win her ear. But as for Odysseus, no matter what wanderers or vagrants say, he will never return — dogs, or wild birds, or the fishes of the deep have devoured his body ere this. Never again shall I find so good a lord, nor would I find one so kind even if I were back in my own land, and saw the faces of my father and my mother. But not so much for them do I mourn as for the loss of my master."

Said Odysseus, "Thou sayst that thy master will never return, but I notice that thou art slow to believe thine own words. Now I tell thee that Odysseus will return and in this same year. And as sure as the old moon wanes and the young moon is born, he will take vengeance on those whom you have spoken of — those who eat his substance and dishonor his wife and son. I say that, and I swear it with an oath."

"I do not heed thine oath," said Eumæus the swineherd. "I do not listen to vagrant's tales about my master since a stranger came here and cheated us with a story. He told us that he had seen Odysseus in the land of the Cretans, in the house of the hero Idomeneus, mending his ships that had been broken by the storm, and that he would be here by summer or by harvest time, bringing with him much wealth."

As they were speaking the younger swineherds came

back from the woods, bringing the drove of swine into the courtyard. There was a mighty din whilst the swine were being put into their pens. Supper time came on, and Eumæus and Odysseus and the younger swineherds sat down to a meal. Eumæus carved the swineflesh, giving the best portion to Odysseus whom he treated as the guest of honor. And Odysseus said, "Eumæus, surely thou art counselled by Zeus, seeing thou dost give the best of the meat even to such a one as I."

And Eumæus, thinking Odysseus was praising him for treating a stranger kindly, said, "Eat, stranger, and make merry with such fare as is here."

The night came on cold with rain. Then Odysseus, to test the kindliness of the swineherd, said, "O that I were young and could endure this bitter night! O that I were better off! Then would one of you swineherds give me a wrap to cover myself from the wind and rain! But now, verily, I am an outcast because of my sorry raiment."

Then Eumæus sprang up and made a bed for Odysseus near the fire. Odysseus lay down, and the swineherd covered him with a mantle he kept for a covering when great storms should arise. Then, that he might better guard the swine, Eumæus, wrapping himself up in a cloak, and taking with him a sword and javelin, to drive off wild beasts should they come near, went to lie nearer to the pens.

When morning came, Odysseus said, "I am going to the town to beg, so that I need take nothing more from thee. Send someone with me to be a guide. I would go to the house of Odysseus, and see if I can earn a little from the wooers who are there. Right well could I serve them if they would take me on. There could be no better serving-man than I, when it comes to splitting faggots, and kindling a fire and carving meat."

"Nay, nay," said Eumæus, "do not go there, stranger. None here are at a loss by thy presence. Stay until the son of Odysseus, Telemachus, returns, and he will do something for thee. Go not near the wooers. It is not such a one as thee that they would have to serve them. Stay this day with us."

Odysseus did not go to the town but stayed all day with Eumæus. And at night, when he and Eumæus and the younger swineherds were seated at the fire, Odysseus said, "Thou, too, Eumæus, hast wandered far and hast had many sorrows. Tell us how thou camest to be a slave and a swineherd."

THE STORY OF EUMÆUS THE SWINEHERD

THERE is," said Eumæus, "a certain island over against Ortygia. That island has two cities, and my father was king over them both.

"There came to the city where my father dwelt, a ship with merchants from the land of the Phœnicians. I was a child then, and there was in my father's house a Phœnician slave-woman who nursed me. Once, when she was washing clothes, one of the sailors from the Phœnician ship spoke to her and asked her would she like to go back with them to their own land.

"She spoke to that sailor and told him her story. 'I am from Sidon in the Phœnician land,' she said, 'and my father was named Artybas, and was famous for his riches. Sea robbers caught me one day as I was crossing the fields, and they stole me away, and brought me here, and sold me to the master of yonder house.'

"Then the sailor said to her, 'Your father and mother are still alive, I know, and they have lost none of their wealth. Wilt thou not come with us and see them again?'

"Then the woman made the sailors swear that they would bring her safely to the city of Sidon. She told them that when their ship was ready she would come down to it, and that she would bring what gold she could lay her hands on away from her master's house, and that she would also bring the child whom she nursed. 'He is a wise child,' she said, 'and you can sell him for a slave when you come to a foreign land.'

"When the Phœnician ship was ready to depart they sent a message to the woman. The sailor who brought the message brought too a chain of gold with amber beads strung here and there, for my mother to buy. And, while my mother and her handmaids were handling the chain, the sailor nodded to the woman, and she went out, taking with her three cups of gold, and leading me by the hand.

"The sun sank and all the ways were darkened. But the Phœnician woman went down to the harbor and came to the ship and went aboard it. And when the sailor who had gone to my father's house came back, they raised the mast and sails, and took the oars in their hands, and drew the ship away from our land. We sailed away and I was left stricken at heart. For six days we sailed over the sea, and on the seventh day the woman died and her body was cast into the deep. The wind and the waves bore us to Ithaka, and there the merchants sold me to Laertes, the father of Odysseus.

"The wife of Laertes reared me kindly, and I grew up with the youngest of her daughters, the lovely Ctimene. But Ctimene went to Same, and was married to one of the princes of that island. Afterwards Laertes' lady sent me to work in the fields. But always she treated me kindly. Now Laertes' lady is dead — she wasted away from grief when she heard no tidings of her only son, Odysseus. Laertes yet lives, but since the death of his noble wife he never leaves his house. All day he sits by his fire, they say, and thinks upon his son's doom, and how his son's substance is being wasted, and how his son's son will have but little to inherit."

So Odysseus passed part of the night, Eumæus telling him of his wanderings and his sorrows. And while they were speaking, Telemachus, the son of Odysseus, came to Ithaka in his good ship. Antinous had lain in wait for him, and had posted sentinels to watch for his ship; nevertheless Telemachus had passed by without being seen by his enemies. And having come to Ithaka, he bade one of his comrades bring the ship into the wharf of the city while he himself went to another place. Leaving the ship he came to the dwelling of the servant he most trusted — to the dwelling of Eumæus, the swineherd.

IX

ON the morning of his fourth day in Ithaka, as he and the swineherd were eating a meal together, Odysseus heard the sound of footsteps approaching the hut. The fierce dogs were outside and he expected to hear them yelping against the stranger's approach. No sound came from them. Then he saw a young man come to the entrance of the courtyard, the swineherd's dogs fawning upon him.

When Eumæus saw this young man he let fall the vessels he was carrying, and running to him, kissed his head and his eyes and his hands. While he was kissing and weeping over him, Odysseus heard the swineherd saying:

"Telemachus, art thou come back to us? Like a light in the darkness thou hast appeared! I thought that never again should we see thee when I heard that thou hadst taken a ship to Pylos! Come in, dear son, come in, that I may see thee once again in mine house."

Odysseus raised his head and looked at his son. As a lion might look over his cub so he looked over Telemachus. But neither the swineherd nor Telemachus was aware of Odysseus' gaze.

"I have come to see thee, friend Eumæus," said Telemachus, "for before I go into the City I would know whether my mother is still in the house of Odysseus, or whether one of the wooers has at last taken her as a wife to his own house."

"Thy mother is still in thy father's house," Eumæus answered. Then Telemachus came within the courtyard. Odysseus in the guise of the old beggar rose from his seat, but the young man said to him courteously: "Be seated, friend. Another seat can be found for me."

Eumæus strewed green brushwood and spread a fleece upon it, and Telemachus seated himself. Next Eumæus fetched a meal for him — oaten cakes and swine flesh and wine. While they were eating, the swineherd said:

"We have here a stranger who has wandered through many countries, and who has come to my house as a suppliant. Wilt thou take him for thy man, Telemachus?"

Said Telemachus, "How can I support any man? I have not the strength of hand to defend mine own house. But for this stranger I will do what I can. I will give him a mantle and doublet, with shoes for his feet and a sword to defend himself, and I will send him on whatever way he wants to go. But, Eumæus, I would not have him go near my father's house. The wooers grow more insolent each day, and they might mock the stranger if he went amongst them."

Then said Odysseus, speaking for the first time, "Young sir, what thou hast said seems strange to me. Dost thou willingly submit to insolence in thine own father's house?

But perhaps it is that the people of the City hate thee and will not help thee against thine enemies. Ah, if I had such youth as I have spirit, or if I were the son of Odysseus, I should go amongst them this very day, and make myself the bane of each man of them. I would rather die in mine own halls than see such shame as is reported — strangers mocked at, and servants injured, and wine and food wasted."

Said Telemachus, "The people of the City do not hate me, and they would help me if they could. But the wooers of my mother are powerful men — men to make the City folk afraid. And if I should oppose them I would assuredly be slain in my father's house, for how could I hope to overcome so many?"

"What wouldst thou have me do for thee, Telemachus?" said the swineherd.

"I would have thee go to my mother, friend Eumæus," Telemachus said, "and let her know that I am safe-returned from Pylos."

Eumæus at once put sandals upon his feet and took his staff in his hands. He begged Telemachus to rest himself in the hut, and then he left the courtyard and went toward the City.

Telemachus lay down on his seat and closed his eyes in weariness. He saw, while thinking that he only dreamt it, a woman come to the gate of the courtyard. She was fair and tall and splendid, and the dogs shrank away from her presence with a whine. She touched the beggar with a golden wand. As she did, the marks of age and beggary fell from him and the man stood up as tall and noble looking.

"Who art thou?" cried Telemachus, starting up. "Even a moment ago thou didst look aged and a beggar! Now thou dost look a chief of men! Art thou one of the divine ones?"

Odysseus looked upon him and said, "My son, do not speak so to me. I am Odysseus, thy father. After much suffering and much wandering I have come to my own country." He kissed his son with tears flowing down his cheeks, and Telemachus threw his arms around his father's neck, but scarce believing that the father he had searched for was indeed before him.

But no doubt was left as Odysseus talked to him, and told him how he had come to Ithaka in a ship given him by the Phæacians, and how he had brought with him gifts of bronze and raiment that were hidden in the cave, and told him, too, how Pallas Athene had changed his appearance into that of an old beggar.

And when his own story was finished he said, "Come, my son, tell me of the wooers who waste the substance of our house — tell me how many they number, and who they are, so that we may prepare a way of dealing with them."

"Even though thou art a great warrior, my father, thou and I cannot hope to deal with them. They have come, not from Ithaka alone, but from all the islands around — from Dulichium and Same and Zacynthus. We two cannot deal with such a throng."

Said Odysseus, "I shall make a plan to deal with them. Go thou home, and keep company with the wooers. Later in the day the swineherd will lead me into the city, and I shall go into the house in the likeness of an old beggar. And if thou shouldst see any of the wooers ill-treat me, harden thine heart to endure it — even if they drag me by the feet to the door of the house, keep quiet thou. And let no one — not even thy mother, Penelope — nor my father Laertes — know that Odysseus hath returned."

Telemachus said, "My father, thou shalt learn soon what spirit is in me and what wisdom I have."

While they talked together the ship that Antinous had taken, when he went to lie in wait for Telemachus, returned. The wooers assembled and debated whether they should kill Telemachus, for now there was danger that he would draw the people to his side, and so make up a force that could drive the wooers out of Ithaka. But they did not agree to kill him then, for there was one amongst them who was against the deed.

Eumæus brought the news to Telemachus and Odysseus of the return of Antinous' ship. He came back to the hut in the afternoon. Pallas Athene had again given Odysseus the appearance of an ancient beggar-man and the swineherd saw no change in his guest.

X

IT was time for Telemachus to go into the City. He put his sandals on his feet, and took his spear in his hand, and then speaking to the swineherd he said:

"Friend Eumæus, I am now going into the City to show myself to my mother, and to let her hear from my own lips the tale of my journey. And I have an order to leave with thee. Take this stranger into the City, that he may go about as he desires, asking alms from the people."

Odysseus in the guise of a beggar said, "I thank thee, lord Telemachus. I would not stay here, for I am not of an age to wait about a hut and courtyard, obeying the orders of a master, even if that master be as good a man as thy swineherd. Go thy way, lord Telemachus, and Eumæus, as thou hast bidden him, will lead me into the City."

Telemachus then passed out of the courtyard and went the ways until he came into the City. When he went into the house, the first person he saw was his nurse, old Eurycleia, who welcomed him with joy. To Eurycleia he spoke of the guest who had come on his ship, Theoclymenus. He told her that this guest would be in the house that day, and that he was to be treated with all honor and reverence. The wooers came into the hall and crowded around him, with fair words in their mouths. Then all sat down at tables, and Eurycleia brought wheaten bread and wine and dainties.

Just at that time Odysseus and Eumæus were journeying toward the City. Odysseus, in the guise of a beggar, had a ragged bag across his shoulders and he carried a staff that the swineherd had given him to help him over the slippery ground. They went by a rugged path and they came to a place where a spring flowed into a basin made for its water, and where there was an altar to the Nymphs, at which men made offerings.

As Eumæus and Odysseus were resting at the spring, a servant from Odysseus' house came along. He was a goatherd, and Melanthius was his name. He was leading a flock of goats for the wooers to kill, and when he saw the swineherd with the seeming beggar he cried out:

"Now we see the vile leading the vile. Say, swineherd, whither art thou leading this wretch? It is easy to see the sort of fellow he is! He is the sort to rub shoulders against many doorposts, begging for scraps. Nothing else is he good for. But if thou wouldst give him to me, swineherd, I would make him watch my fields, and sweep out my stalls, and carry fresh water to the kids. He'd have his dish of whey from me. But a fellow like this doesn't want an honest job — he wants to lounge through the country, filling his belly, without doing anything for the people who feed him up. If he goes to the house of Odysseus, I pray that he be pelted from the door."

He said all this as he came up to them with his flock of goats. And as he went by he gave a kick to Odysseus.

Odysseus took thought whether he should strike the

fellow with his staff or fling him upon the ground. But in the end he hardened his heart to endure the insult, and let the goatherd go on his way. But turning to the altar that was by the spring, he prayed:

"Nymphs of the Well! If ever Odysseus made offerings to you, fulfil for me this wish — that he — even Odysseus — may come to his own home, and have power to chastise the insolence that gathers around his house."

They journeyed on, and when they came near they heard the sound of the lyre within the house. The wooers were now feasting, and Phemius the minstrel was singing to them. And when Odysseus came before his own house, he caught the swineherd by the hand suddenly and with a hard grip, and he said:

"Lo now, I who have wandered in many lands and have walked in pain through many Cities have come at last to the house of Odysseus. There it is, standing as of old, with building beyond building; with its walls and its battlements; its courts and its doors. The house of Odysseus, verily! And lo! Unwelcome men keep reveal within it, and the smoke of their feast rises up and the sound of the lyre is heard playing for them."

Said Eumæus, "What wilt thou have me do for thee, friend? Shall I bring thee into the hall and before the company of wooers, whilst I remain here, or wouldst thou have me go in before thee?"

"I would have thee go in before me," Odysseus said.

Now as they went through the courtyard a thing happened that dashed Odysseus' eyes with tears. A hound lay in the dirt of the yard, a hound that was very old. All uncared for he lay in the dirt, old and feeble. But he had been a famous hound, and Odysseus himself had trained him before he went to the wars of Troy. Argos was his name. Now as Odysseus came near, the hound Argos knew him, and stood up before him and whined and dropped his ears, but had no strength to come near him. Odysseus knew the hound and stopped and gazed at him. "A good hound lies there," said he to Eumæus, "once, I think, he was so swift that no beast in the deep places of the wood could flee from him." Then he went on, and the hound Argos lay down in the dirt of the yard, and that same day the life passed from him.

Behind Eumæus, the swineherd, he came into his own hall, in the appearance of a beggar, wretchedly clad and leaning on an old man's staff. Odysseus looked upon the young lords who wooed his wife, and then he sat upon the threshold and went no further into the hall.

Telemachus was there. Seeing Eumæus he called to him and gave the swineherd bread and meat, and said, "Take these, and give them to the stranger at the doorway, and tell him that he may go amongst the company and crave an alms from each."

Odysseus ate whilst the minstrel was finishing his song. When it was finished he rose up, and went into the hall, craving an alms from each of the wooers.

Seeing him, Antinous, the most insolent of the wooers, cried out, "O notorious swineherd, why didst thou bring this fellow here? Have we not enough vagabonds? Is it

nothing to thee that worthless fellows come here and devour thy master's substance?"

Hearing such a speech from Antinous, Telemachus had to say, "Antinous, I see that thou hast good care for me and mine. I marvel that thou hast such good care. But wouldst thou have me drive a stranger from the door? The gods forbid that I should do such a thing. Nay, Antinous. Give the stranger something for the sake of the house."

"If all the company gives him as much as I, he will have something to keep him from beggary for a three months' space," said Antinous, meaning by that that he would work some hurt upon the beggar.

Odysseus came before him. "They say that thou art the noblest of all the wooers," he said, "and for that reason thou shouldst give me a better thing than any of the others have given me. Look upon me. I too had a house of mine own, and was accounted wealthy amongst men, and I had servants to wait upon me. And many a time would I make welcome the wanderer and give him something from my store."

"Stand far away from my table, thou wretched fellow," said Antinous.

Then said Odysseus, "Thou hast beauty, lord Antinous, but thou hast not wisdom. Out of thine own house thou wouldst not give a grain of salt to a suppliant. And even whilst thou dost sit at another man's table thou dost not find it in thy heart to give something out of the plenty that is before thee."

So Odysseus spoke and Antinous became terribly angered. He caught up a footstool, and with it he struck Odysseus in the back, at the base of the right shoulder. Such a blow would have knocked another man over, but Odysseus stood steadfast under it. He gave one look at Antinous, and then without a word he went over and sat down again upon the threshold.

Telemachus had in his heart a mighty rage for the stroke that had been given his father. But he let no tear fall from his eyes and he sat very still, brooding in his heart evil for the wooers. Odysseus, after a while, lifted his head and spoke:

"Wooers of the renowned queen," he said, "hear what the spirit within me bids me say to you. There is neither pain nor shame in the blow that a man may get in battle. But in the blow that Antinous has given me — a blow aimed at a beggar — there is pain and there is shame. And now I call upon the god who is the avenger of the insult to the poor, to bring, not a wedding to Antinous, but the issue of death."

"Sit there and eat thy meat in quiet," Antinous called out, "or else thou wilt be dragged through the house by thy heels, and the flesh will be stripped off thy bones."

And now the lady Penelope had come into the hall. Hearing that a stranger was there, she sent for Eumæus and bade the swineherd bring him to her, that she might question him as to what he had heard about Odysseus. Eumæus came and told him of Penelope's request. But Odysseus said, "Eumæus, right willing am I to tell the truth about Odysseus to the fair and wise Penelope. But now I may not speak to her. Go to her and tell her that when the wooers have gone I will speak to her. And ask her to give me a seat near the fire, that I may sit and warm myself as I speak, for the clothes I wear are comfortless."

As Eumæus gave the message to the lady Penelope, one who was there, Theoclymenus, the guest who had come in Telemachus' ship, said, "O wife of the renowned Odysseus, be sure that thy lord will return to his house. As I came here on the ship of Telemachus, thy son, I saw a happening that is an omen of the return of Odysseus. A bird flew out on the right, a hawk. In his talons he held a dove, and plucked her and shed the feathers down on the ship. By that omen I know that the lord of this high house will return, and strike here in his anger."

Penelope left the hall and went back to her own chamber. Next Eumæus went away to look after his swine. But still the wooers continued to feast, and still Odysseus sat in the guise of a beggar on the threshold of his own house.

XI

THERE was in Ithaka a common beggar; he was a most greedy fellow, and he was nicknamed Irus because he used to run errands for the servants of Odysseus' house. He came in the evening, and seeing a seeming beggar seated on the threshold, he flew into a rage and shouted at him:

"Get away from here, old fellow, lest you be dragged away by the hand or foot. Look you! The lords within the house are giving me the wink to turn you out. But I can't demean myself by touching the like of you. Get up now and go while I'm easy with you."

Odysseus looked at the fellow and said, "I have not harmed you in deed or word, and I do not grudge you anything of what you may get in this house. The threshold I sit on is wide enough for two of us."

"What words this fellow has!" said Irus the beggar. "He talks like an old sit-by-the-fire. I'll not waste more words on him. Get up now, heavy paunch, and strip for the fight, for I'm going to show all the lords that I can keep the door for them."

"Do not provoke me," said Odysseus. "Old as I seem, I may be able to draw your blood."

But Irus kept on shouting, "I'll knock the teeth out of your jaws." "I'll trounce you." Antinous, the most insolent of the wooers, saw the squabble, and he laughed to see the pair defying each other. "Friends," said he, "the gods are good to us, and don't fail to send us amusement. The strange beggar and our own Irus are threatening each other. Let us see that they don't draw back from the fight. Let us match one against the other."

All the wooers trooped to the threshold and stood round the ragged men. Antinous thought of something to make the game more merry. "There are two great puddings in the larder," he said. "Let us offer them for a prize to these pugilists. Come, Irus. Come, stranger. A choice of puddings for whichever of you wins the match. Aye, and more than that. Whoever wins shall have leave to eat every day in this hall, and no other beggar shall be let come near the house. Go to it now, ye mighty men." All the wooers crowded round and clapped the men on to the fight.

Odysseus said, "Friends, an old man like me cannot fight one who is younger and abler."

But they cried to him, "Go on, go on. Get into the fight or else take stripes upon your body."

Then said Odysseus, "Swear to me, all of you, that none of you will show favor to Irus nor deal me a foul blow."

All the wooers cried out that none would favor Irus or deal his opponent a foul blow. And Telemachus, who was there, said, "The man who strikes thee, stranger, will have to take reckoning from me."

Straightway Odysseus girt up his rags. When his great arms and shoulders and thighs were seen, the wooers were amazed and Irus was frightened. He would have slipped away if Antinous had not caught him and said to him, "You lubber, you! If you do not stand up before this man I will have you flung on my ship and sent over to King Echetus, who will cut off your nose and ears and give your flesh to his dogs to eat." He took hold of Irus and dragged him into the ring.

The fighters faced each other. But Odysseus with his hands upraised stood for long without striking, for he was pondering whether he should strike Irus a hard or a light blow. It seemed to him better to strike him lightly, so that his strength should not be made a matter for the wooers to note and wonder at. Irus struck first. He struck Odys-

seus on the shoulder. Then Odysseus aimed a blow at his neck, just below the ear, and the beggar fell to the ground, with the blood gushing from his mouth and nose.

The wooers were not sorry for Irus. They laughed until they were ready to fall backwards. Then Odysseus seized Irus by the feet and dragged him out of the house, and to the gate of the courtyard. He lifted him up and put him standing against the wall. Placing the staff in the beggar's hands, he said, "Sit there, and scare off the dogs and swine, and do not let such a one as you lord it over strangers. A worse thing might have befallen you."

Then back he went to the hall, with his beggar's bag on his shoulder and his clothes more ragged than ever. Back he went, and when the wooers saw him they burst into peals of laughter and shouted out:

"May Zeus, O stranger, give thee thy dearest wish and thy heart's desire. Thou only shalt be beggar in Ithaka." They laughed and laughed again when Antinous brought out the great pudding that was the prize. Odysseus took it from him. And another of the wooers pledged him in a golden cup, saying, "May you come to your own, O beggar, and may happiness be yours in time to come."

While these things were happening, the wife of Odysseus, the lady Penelope, called to Eurycleia, and said, "This evening I will go into the hall of our house and speak to my son, Telemachus. Bid my two handmaidens make ready to come with me, for I shrink from going amongst the wooers alone."

Eurycleia went to tell the handmaidens and Penelope

washed off her cheeks the traces of the tears that she had wept that day. Then she sat down to wait for the handmaidens to come to her. As she waited she fell into a deep sleep. And as she slept, the goddess Pallas Athene bathed her face in the Water of Beauty and took all weariness away from her body, and restored all her youthfulness to her. The sound of the handmaidens' voices as they came in awakened her, and Penelope rose up to go into the hall.

Now when she came amongst them with her two handmaidens, one standing each side of her, the wooers were amazed, for they had never seen one so beautiful. The hearts of all were enchanted with love for her, and each prayed that he might have her for his wife.

Penelope did not look on any of the wooers, but she went to her son, Telemachus, and spoke to him.

"Telemachus," she said, "I have heard that a stranger has been ill-treated in this house. How, my child, didst thou permit such a thing to happen?"

Telemachus said, "My lady mother, thou hast no right to be angered at what took place in this hall."

So they spoke to one another, mother and son. Now one of the wooers, Eurymachus by name, spoke to Penelope, saying:

"Lady, if any more than we beheld thee in the beauty thou hast now, by so many more wouldst thou have wooers tomorrow."

"Speak not so to me, lord Eurymachus," said Penelope, "speak not of my beauty, which departed in the grief I felt when my lord went to the wars of Troy."

Odysseus stood up, and gazed upon his wife who was standing amongst her wooers. Eurymachus noted him and going to him, said, "Stranger, wouldst thou be my hireling? If thou wouldst work on my upland farm, I should give thee food and clothes. But I think thou art practiced only in shifts and dodges, and that thou wouldst prefer to go begging thy way through the country."

Odysseus, standing there, said to that proud wooer, "lord Eurymachus, if there might be a trial of labor between us two, I know which of us would come out the better man. I would that we two stood together, a scythe in the hands of each, and a good swath of meadow to be mown — then would I match with thee, fasting from dawn until evening's dark. Or would that we were set ploughing together. Then thou shouldst see who would plough the longest and the best furrow! Or would that we two were in the ways of war! Then shouldst thou see who would be in the front rank of battle. Thou didst think thyself a great man. But if Odysseus should return, that door, wide as it is, would be too narrow for thy flight."

So angry was Eurymachus at this speech that he would have struck Odysseus if Telemachus had not come amongst the wooers, saying, "That man must not be struck again in this hall. Sirs, if you have finished feasting, and if the time has come for you, go to your own homes, go in peace I pray you."

All were astonished that Telemachus should speak so boldly. No one answered him back, for one said to the other, "What he has said is proper. We have nothing to say against it. To misuse a stranger in the house of Odysseus is a shame. Now let us pour out a libation of wine to the gods, and then let each man go to his home."

The wine was poured out and the wooers departed. Then Penelope and her handmaidens went to her own chamber and Telemachus was left with his father, Odysseus.

XII

TO Telemachus Odysseus said, "My son, we must now get the weapons out of the hall. Take them down from the walls." Telemachus and his father took down the helmets and shields and sharp-pointed spears. Then said Odysseus as they carried them out, "Tomorrow, when the wooers miss the weapons and say, 'Why have they been taken?' answer them, saying, 'The smoke of the fire dulled them, and they no longer looked the weapons that my father left behind him when he went to the wars of Troy. Besides, I am fearful lest some day the company in the hall come to a quarrel, one with the other, and snatch the weapons in anger. Strife has come here already. And iron draws iron, men say.' "

Telemachus carried the armor and weapons out of the hall and hid them in the women's apartment. Then when the hall was cleared he went to his own chamber.

It was then that Penelope came back to the hall to speak

to the stranger. One of her handmaidens, Melantho by name, was there, and she was speaking angrily to him. Now this Melantho was proud and hard of heart because Antinous often conversed with her. As Penelope came near she was saying:

"Stranger, art thou still here, prying things out and spying on the servants? Be thankful for the supper thou hast gotten and betake thyself out of this."

Odysseus, looking fiercely at her, said, "Why shouldst thou speak to me in such a way? If I go in ragged clothes and beg through the land it is because of my necessity. Once I had a house with servants and with much substance, and the stranger who came there was not abused."

The lady Penelope called to the handmaiden and said, "Thou, Melantho, didst hear it from mine own lips that I was minded to speak to this stranger and ask him if he had tidings of my lord. Therefore, it does not become thee to revile him." She spoke to the old nurse who had come with her, and said, "Eurycleia, bring to the fire a bench, with a fleece upon it, that this stranger may sit and tell me his story."

Eurycleia brought over the bench, and Odysseus sat down near the fire. Then said the lady Penelope, "First, stranger, wilt thou tell me who thou art, and what is thy name, and thy race and thy country?"

Said Odysseus, "Ask me all thou wilt, lady, but inquire not concerning my name, or race, or country, lest thou shouldst fill my heart with more pains than I am able to endure. Verily I am a man of grief. But hast thou no tale to tell me? We know of thee, Penelope, for thy fame goes up to heaven, and no one of mortal men can find fault with thee."

Then said Penelope, "What excellence I had of face or form departed from me when my lord Odysseus went from this hall to the wars of Troy. And since he went a host of ills has beset me. Ah, would that he were here to watch over my life! The lords of all the islands around — Dulichium and Same and Zacynthus; and the lords of the land of Ithaka, have come here and are wooing me against my will. They devour the substance of this house and my son is being impoverished.

"Long ago a god put into my mind a device to keep marriage with any of them away from me. I set up a great web upon my loom and I spoke to the wooers, saying, 'Odysseus is assuredly dead, but I crave that you be not eager to speed on this marriage with me. Wait until I finish the web I am weaving. It is a shroud for Odysseus' father, and I make it against the day when death shall come to him. There will be no woman to care for Laertes when I have left his son's house, and I would not have such a hero lie without a shroud, lest the women of our land should blame me for neglect of my husband's father in his last days.'

"So I spoke, and they agreed to wait until the web was woven. In the daytime I wove it, but at night I unravelled the web. So three years passed away. Then the fourth year came, and my wooers were hard to deal with. My treacherous handmaidens brought them upon me as I was unravelling the web. And now I cannot devise any other plan to keep the marriage away from me. My parents command me to marry one of my wooers. My son cannot long endure to see the substance of his house and field being wasted, and the wealth that should be his destroyed. He too would wish that I should marry. And there is no reason why I should not be wed again, for surely Odysseus, my lord, is dead."

Said Odysseus, "Thy lord was known to me. On his way to Troy he came to my land, for the wind blew him out of his course, sending him wandering past Malea. For twelve days he stayed in my city, and I gave him good entertainment, and saw that he lacked for nothing in cattle, or wine, or barley meal."

When Odysseus was spoken of, the heart of Penelope melted, and tears ran down her cheeks. Odysseus had pity for his wife when he saw her weeping for the man who was even then sitting by her. Tears would have run down his own cheeks only that he was strong enough to hold them back.

Said Penelope, "Stranger, I cannot help but question thee about Odysseus. What raiment had he on when thou didst see him? And what men were with him?"

Said Odysseus, "Lady, it is hard for one so long parted from him to tell thee what thou hast asked. It is now twenty years since I saw Odysseus. He wore a purple mantle that was fastened with a brooch. And this brooch had on it the image of a hound holding a fawn between its forepaws. All the people marvelled at this brooch, for it was of gold, and the fawn and the hound were done to the life. And I remember that there was a henchman with Odysseus — he was a man somewhat older than his master, round shouldered and black-skinned and curly headed. His name was Eurybates, and Odysseus honored him above the rest of his company."

When he spoke, giving such tokens of Odysseus, Penelope wept again. And when she had wept for a long time she said:

"Stranger, thou wert made welcome, but now thou shalt be honored in this hall. Thou dost speak of the garments that Odysseus wore. It was I who gave him these garments, folding them myself and bringing them out of the chamber. And it was I who gave him the brooch that thou hast described. Ah, it was an evil fate that took him from me, bringing him to Troy, that place too evil to be named by me."

Odysseus leaned toward her, and said, "Do not waste thy heart with endless weeping, lady. Cease from lamentation, and lay up in thy mind the word I give thee. Odysseus is near. He has lost all his companions, and he knows not how to come into this house, whether openly or by stealth. I swear it. By the hearth of Odysseus to which I am come, I swear that Odysseus himself will stand up here before the old moon wanes and the new moon is born."

"Ah, no," said Penelope. "Often before have wanderers told me such comfortable things, and I believed them. I know now that thy word cannot be accomplished. But it is time for thee to rest thyself, stranger. My handmaidens will make a bed for thee in the vestibule, and then come to thee and bathe thy feet."

Said Odysseus, "Thy handmaidens would be loath to touch the feet of a wanderer such as I. But if there is in the house some old wife who has borne such troubles as I have borne, I would have my feet bathed by her."

Said Penelope, "Here is an ancient woman who nursed and tended that hapless man, Odysseus. She took him in her arms in the very hour he was born. Eurycleia, wash the feet of this man, who knew thy lord and mine."

Thereupon the nurse, old Eurycleia, fetched water, both hot and cold, and brought the bath to the hearth. And standing before Odysseus in the flickering light of the fire, she said, "I will wash thy feet, both for Penelope's sake and for thine own. The heart within me is moved at the sight of thee. Many strangers have come into this hall, but I have never seen one that was so like as thou art to Odysseus."

Said Odysseus, "Many people have said that Odysseus and I favor each other."

His feet were in the water, and she put her hand upon one of them. As she did so, Odysseus turned his face away to the darkness, for it suddenly came into his mind that his nurse, old Eurycleia, might recognize the scar that was upon that foot.

How came it there, that scar? It had been made long ago when a boar's tusk had ripped up the flesh of his foot. Odysseus was then a youth, and he had gone to the mountain Parnassus to visit there his mother's father.

One morning, with his uncles, young Odysseus went up the slope of the mountain Parnassus, to hunt with hounds. In a thick lair a mighty boar was lying. When the sound of the men's trampling came near him, he sprang up with gleaming eyes and stood before them all. Odysseus, holding his spear in his hands, rushed upon him. But before he could strike him, the boar charged, ripping deep into his flesh with his tusk. Then Odysseus speared him through the shoulder and the boar was slain. His uncles staunched the wound and he stayed with them on the mountain Parnassus, in his grandfather's house, until the wound was healed.

And now, as Eurycleia, his old nurse, passed her hands along the leg, she let his foot drop suddenly. His knee struck against the bath, and the vessel of water was overturned. The nurse touched the chin of Odysseus and she said, "Thou art Odysseus."

She looked to where Penelope was sitting, so that she might make a sign to her. But Penelope had her eyes turned away. Odysseus put his hand on Eurycleia's mouth, and with the other hand he drew her to him.

"Woman," he whispered, "Say nothing. Be silent, lest mine enemies learn what thou knowest now."

"Silent I'll be," said the nurse Eurycleia. "Thou knowest me. Firm and unyielding I am, and by no sign will I let anyone know that thou hast come under this roof."

So saying she went out of the hall to fetch water in the place of that which had been spilt. She came back and finished bathing his feet. Then Odysseus arranged the rags around his leg to hide the scar, and he drew the bench closer to the fire.

Penelope turned to him again. "Wise thou art, my guest," she said, "and it may be that thou art just such a man as can interpret a dream that comes to me constantly. I have twenty geese in the yard outside. In my dream I see them, and then a great eagle flies down from the mountains, and breaks their necks and kills them all, and lays them in a heap in this hall. I weep and lament for my geese, but then the eagle comes back, and perching on a beam of the roof speaks to me in the voice of a man. 'Take heart, O wife of Odysseus,' the eagle says, 'this is no dream but a true vision. For the geese that thou hast seen are thy wooers, and I, that appeared as an eagle, am thy husband who will swiftly bring death to the wooers.' Then the dream goes, and I waken and look out on the daylight and see my geese in the courtyard pecking at the wheat in the trough. Canst thou interpret this dream?"

"Lady," said Odysseus, "the dream interprets itself. All will come about as thou hast dreamed."

"Ah," said Penelope, "but it cannot now, for the day of my woe is at hand. I am being forced by my parents to choose a husband from the wooers, and depart from the house of Odysseus."

"And how wilt thou choose from amongst them?" said Odysseus.

"In this way will I make choice," said Penelope. "My husband's great bow is still in the house. The one who can bend that bow, and shoot an arrow through the holes in the backs of twelve axes set one behind the other — him will I choose for my husband."

Said Odysseus, "Thy device is good, Penelope, and some god hath instructed thee to do this. But delay no longer the contest of the bow. Let it be tomorrow."

"Is that thy counsel, O stranger?" said Penelope.

"It is my counsel," said Odysseus.

"I thank thee for thy counsel," she said. "And now farewell, for I must go to my rest. And do thou lie down in the vestibule, in the bed that has been made for thee."

So Penelope spoke, and then she went to her chamber with her handmaidens. And in her bed she thought over all the stranger had told her of Odysseus, and she wept again for him.

XIII

ALL night Odysseus lay awake, tossing this side and that, as he pondered on how he might slay the wooers, and save his house from them. As soon as the dawn came, he went into the open air and, lifting up his hands, prayed to Zeus, the greatest of the gods, that he might be shown some sign, as to whether he would win victory or meet with defeat.

And then, as he was going within the house, he heard the voice of a woman who ground barley meal between stones. She was one of twelve, but the other women had fallen asleep by the quernstones. She was an ancient, wretched woman, covered all over with the dust of the grain, and, as Odysseus came near her, she lifted up her hands and prayed in a weak voice:

"O Zeus, even for miserable me, fulfil a prayer! May this be the last day that the wooers make their feast in the house of Odysseus! They have loosened my knees with the cruel toil they have made me undergo, grinding for them the barley for the bread they eat. O Zeus, may they today sup their last!"

Thus the quern-woman spoke, as Odysseus crossed his threshold. He was glad of her speech, for it seemed to him her words were an omen from Zeus, and that vengeance would soon be wrought upon the proud and hardhearted men who wasted the goods of the house and oppressed the servants.

And now the maids came into the hall from the women's apartment, and some cleaned the tables and others took pitchers and went to the well for water. Then menservants came in and split the fagots for the fire. Other servants came into the courtyard — Eumæus the swineherd, driving fatted swine, the best of his drove, and Philœtius the cattleherd bringing a calf. The goatherd Melanthius, him whom Odysseus and Eumæus had met on the road the day before, also came, bringing the best goats of his flock to be killed for the wooers' feast.

When the cattleherd, Philœtius, saw a stranger in the guise of a beggar, he called out as he tethered the calf in the yard. "Hail, stranger friend! My eyes fill with tears as

I look on thee. For even now, clad as thou art in rags, thou dost make me think of my master Odysseus, who may be a wanderer such as thou in friendless lands. Ah, that he might return and make a scattering of the wooers in his hall." Eumæus the swineherd came up to Philœtius and made the same prayer. These two, and the ancient woman at the quern, were the only ones of his servants whom he heard pray for his return.

And now the wooers came into the hall. Philœtius the cattleherd, and Melanthius the evil goatherd, went amongst them, handing them bread and meat and wine. Odysseus stood outside the hall until Telemachus went to him and brought him within.

Now there was amongst the wooers a man named Ctesippus, and he was the rudest and the roughest of them all. When he saw Telemachus bringing Odysseus within he shouted out, "Here is a guest of Telemachus to whom some gift is due from us. It will be unseemly if he should get nothing today. Therefore I will bestow this upon him as a token."

Saying this, Ctesippus took up the foot of a slaughtered ox and flung it full at Odysseus. Odysseus drew back, and the ox's foot struck the wall. Then did Odysseus smile grimly upon the wooers.

Said Telemachus, "Verily, Ctesippus, the cast turned out happily for thyself. For if thou shouldst have struck my guest, there would have been a funeral feast instead of a wedding banquet in thy father's house. Assuredly I should have driven my spear through thee."

All the wooers were silent when Telemachus spoke these bold words. But soon they fell laughing at something one of their number said. The guest from Telemachus' ship, Theoclymenus, was there, and he started up and went to leave the hall.

"Why dost thou go, my guest?" said Telemachus.

"I see the walls and the beams of the roof sprinkled with blood," said Theoclymenus, the second-sighted man. "I hear the voice of wailing. I see cheeks wet with tears. The men before me have shrouds upon them. The courtyard is filled with ghosts."

So Theoclymenus spoke, and all the wooers laughed at the second-sighted man, for he stumbled about the hall as if it were in darkness. Then said one of the wooers, "Lead that man out of the house, for surely he cannot tell day from night."

"I will go from the place," said Theoclymenus. "I see death approaching. Not one of all the company before me will be able to avoid it."

So saying, the second-sighted man went out of the hall. The wooers looking at each other laughed again, and one of them said:

"Telemachus has no luck in his guests. One is a dirty beggar, who thinks of nothing but what he can put from his hand into his mouth, and the other wants to stand up here and play the seer." So the wooers spake in mockery, but neither Telemachus nor Odysseus paid heed to their words, for their minds were bent upon the time when they should take vengeance upon them.

XIV

IN the treasure chamber of the house Odysseus' great bow was kept. That bow had been given to him by a hero named Iphitus long ago. Odysseus had not taken it with him when he went to the wars of Troy.

To the treasure chamber Penelope went. She carried in her hand the great key that opened the doors — a key all of bronze with a handle of ivory. Now as she thrust the key into the locks, the doors groaned as a bull groans. She went within, and saw the great bow upon its peg. She took it down and laid it upon her knees, and thought long upon the man who had bent it.

Beside the bow was its quiver full of bronze-weighted arrows. The servant took the quiver and Penelope took the bow, and they went from the treasure chamber and into the hall where the wooers were.

When she came in she spoke to the company and said: "Lords of Ithaka and of the islands around: You have come here, each desiring that I should wed him. Now the time has come for me to make my choice of a man from amongst you. Here is how I shall make choice."

"This is the bow of Odysseus, my lord who is no more. Whosoever amongst you who can bend this bow and shoot an arrow from it through the holes in the backs of twelve axes which I shall have set up, him will I wed, and to his house I will go, forsaking the house of my wedlock, this house so filled with treasure and substance, this house which I shall remember in my dreams."

As she spoke Telemachus took the twelve axes and set them upright in an even line, so that one could shoot an arrow through the hole that was in the back of each axe-head. Then Eumæus, the old swineherd, took the bow of Odysseus, and laid it before the wooers.

One of the wooers took up the bow and tried to bend it. But he could not bend it, and he laid it down at the door-way with the arrow beside it. The others took up the bow, and warmed it at the fire, and rubbed it with lard to make it more pliable. As they were doing this, Eumæus, the swineherd, and Philœtius, the cattleherd, passed out of the hall.

Odysseus followed them into the courtyard. He laid a hand on each and said, "Swineherd and cattleherd, I have a word to say to you. But will you keep it to yourselves, the word I say? And first, what would you do to help Odysseus if he should return? Would you stand on his side, or on the side of the wooers? Answer me now from your hearts."

Said Philœtius the cattleherd, "May Zeus fulfil my wish and bring Odysseus back! Then thou shouldst know on whose side I would stand." And Eumæus said, "If Odysseus should return I would be on his side, and that with all the strength that is in me."

When they said this, Odysseus declared himself. Lifting

up his hand to heaven he said, "I am your master, Odysseus. After twenty years I have come back to my own country, and I find that of all my servants, by you two alone is my homecoming desired. If you need see a token that I am indeed Odysseus, look down on my foot. See there the mark that the wild boar left on me in the days of my youth."

Straightway he drew the rags from the scar, and the swineherd and the cattleherd saw it and marked it well. Knowing that it was indeed Odysseus who stood before them, they cast their arms around him and kissed him on the head and shoulders. And Odysseus was moved by their tears, and he kissed their heads and their hands.

As they went back to the hall, he told Eumæus to bring the bow to him as he was bearing it through the hall. He told him, too, to order Eurycleia, the faithful nurse, to bar the doors of the women's apartment at the end of the hall, and to bid the women, even if they heard a groaning and a din, not to come into the hall. And he charged the cattleherd Philœtius to bar the gates of the courtyard.

As he went into the hall, one of the wooers, Eurymachus, was striving to bend the bow. As he struggled to do so he groaned aloud:

"Not because I may not marry Penelope do I groan, but because we youths of today are shown to be weaklings beside Odysseus, whose bow we can in no way bend."

Then Antinous, the proudest of the wooers, made answer and said, "Why should we strive to bend the bow today? Nay, lay the bow aside, Eurymachus, and let the wine-bearers pour us out a cupful each. In the morning let us make sacrifice to the Archer-god, and pray that the bow be fitted to some of our hands."

Then Odysseus came forward and said, "Sirs, you do well to lay the bow aside for today. But will you not put the bow into my hands, that I may try to bend it, and judge for myself whether I have any of the strength that once was mine?"

All the wooers were angry that a seeming beggar should attempt to bend the bow that none of their company were able to bend; Antinous spoke to him sharply and said:

"Thou wretched beggar! Is it not enough that thou art let into this high hall to pick up scraps, but thou must listen to our speech and join in our conversation? If thou shouldst bend that bow we will make short shrift of thee, I promise. We will put thee on a ship and send thee over to King Echetus, who will cut thee to pieces and give thy flesh to his hounds."

Old Eumæus had taken up the bow. As he went with it to Odysseus some of them shouted to him, "Where art thou going with the bow, thou crazy fellow? Put it down." Eumæus was confused by their shouts, and he put down the bow.

Then Telemachus spoke to him and said, "Eumæus, beware of being the man who served many masters." Eumæus, hearing these words, took it up again and brought it to Odysseus, and put the bow into his hands.

As Odysseus stood in the doorway of the hall, the bow in his hands, and with the arrows scattered at his feet,

Eumæus went to Eurycleia, and told her to bar the door of the women's apartment at the back. Then Philœtius, the cattleherd, went out of the hall and barred the gates leading out of the courtyard.

For long Odysseus stood with the bow in his hands, handling it as a minstrel handles a lyre when he stretches a cord or tightens a peg. Then he bent the great bow; he bent it without an effort, and at his touch the bowstring made a sound that was like the cry of a swallow. The wooers seeing him bend that mighty bow felt, every man of them, a sharp pain at the heart. They saw Odysseus take up an arrow and fit it to the string. He held the notch, and he drew the string, and he shot the bronze-weighted arrow straight through the holes in the back of the axe-heads.

Then as Eumæus took up the axes, and brought them outside, he said, "Thou seest, lord Telemachus, that thy guest does not shame thee through foolish boasting. I have bent the bow of Odysseus, and I have shot the arrow aright. But now it is time to provide the feast for the lords who woo thy lady mother. While it is yet light, the feast must be served to them, and with the feast they must have music and the dance."

Saying this he nodded to Telemachus, bending his terrible brows. Telemachus instantly girt his sword upon him and took his spear in his hand. Outside was heard the thunder of Zeus. And now Odysseus had stripped his rags from him and was standing upright, looking a master of men. The mighty bow was in his hands, and at his feet were scattered many bronze-weighted arrows.

XV

IT is ended," Odysseus said, "My trial is ended. Now will I have another mark." Saying this, he put the bronze-weighted arrow against the string of the bow, and shot at the first of his enemies.

It was at Antinous he pointed the arrow — at Antinous who was even then lifting up a golden cup filled with wine, and who was smiling, with death far from his thoughts. Odysseus aimed at him and smote him with the arrow in the throat, and the point passed out clean through his neck. The wine cup fell from his hands and Antinous fell dead across the table. Then did all the wooers raise a shout, threatening Odysseus for sending an arrow astray. It did not come into their minds that this stranger-beggar had aimed to kill Antinous.

But Odysseus shouted back to them, "Ye dogs, ye that said in your hearts that Odysseus would never return to his home, ye that wasted my substance, and troubled my wife, and injured my servants; ye who showed no fear of heaven, nor of the just judgments of men; behold Odysseus returned, and know what death is being loosed on you!"

Then Eurymachus shouted out, "Friends, this man will not hold his hands, nor cease from shooting with the bow, until all of us are slain. Now must we enter into the battle with him. Draw your swords and hold up the tables before you for shields and advance upon him."

But even as he spoke Odysseus, with a terrible cry, loosed an arrow at him and shot Eurymachus through the breast. He let the sword fall from his hand, and he too fell dead upon the floor.

One of the band rushed straight at Odysseus with his sword in hand. But Telemachus was at hand, and he drove his spear through this man's shoulders. Then Telemachus ran quickly to a chamber where there were weapons and armor lying. The swineherd and the cattleherd joined him, and all three put armor upon them. Odysseus, as long as he had arrows to defend himself, kept shooting at and smiting the wooers. When all the arrows were gone, he put the helmet on his head and took up the shield that Telemachus had brought, and the two great spears.

But now Melanthius, the goatherd — he who was the enemy of Odysseus, got into the chamber where the arms were kept, and brought out spears and shields and helmets, and gave them to the wooers. Seeing the goatherd go back for more arms, Telemachus and Eumæus dashed into the chamber, and caught him and bound him with a rope, and dragged him up near the roof-beams, and left him hanging there. Then they closed and bolted the door, and stood on guard.

Many of the wooers lay dead upon the floor of the hall. Now one who was called Agelaus stood forward, and directed the wooers to cast spears at Odysseus. But not one of the spears they cast struck him, for Odysseus was able to avoid them all.

And now he directed Telemachus and Eumæus and Philœtius to cast their spears. When they cast them with Odysseus, each one struck a man, and four of the wooers fell down. And again Odysseus directed his following to cast their spears, and again they cast them, and slew their men. They drove those who remained from one end of the hall to the other, and slew them all.

Straightway the doors of the women's apartment were flung open, and Eurycleia appeared. She saw Odysseus amongst the bodies of the dead, all stained with blood. She would have cried out in triumph if Odysseus had not restrained her. "Rejoice within thine own heart," he said, "but do not cry aloud, for it is an unholy thing to triumph over men lying dead. These men the gods themselves have overcome, because of their own hard and unjust hearts."

As he spoke the women came out of their chambers, carrying torches in their hands. They fell upon Odysseus and embraced him and clasped and kissed his hands. A longing came over him to weep, for he remembered them from of old — every one of the servants who were there.

XVI

EURYCLEIA, the old nurse, went to the upper chamber where Penelope lay in her bed. She bent over her and called out, "Awake, Penelope, dear child. Come down and see with thine own eyes what hath happened. The wooers are overthrown. And he whom thou hast ever longed to see hath come back. Odysseus, thy husband, hath returned. He hath slain the proud wooers who have troubled thee for so long."

But Penelope only looked at the nurse, for she thought that her brain had been turned.

Still Eurycleia kept on saying, "In very deed Odysseus is here. He is that guest whom all the wooers dishonor in the hall."

Then hearing Eurycleia say these words, Penelope sprang out of bed and put her arms round the nurse's neck. "O tell me — if what thou dost say be true — tell me how this stranger slew the wooers, who were so many."

"I did not see the slaying," Eurycleia said, "but I heard the groaning of the men as they were slain. And then I found Odysseus standing amongst many dead men, and it comforted my heart to see him standing there like a lion aroused. Come with me now, lady, that you may both enter into your heart's delight — you that have suffered so much of affliction. Thy lord hath come alive to his own hearth, and he hath found his wife and his son alive and well."

"Ah no!" said Penelope, "ah no, Odysseus hath not returned. He who hath slain the wooers is one of the deathless gods, come down to punish them for their injustice and their hardheartedness. Odysseus long ago lost the way of his returning, and he is lying dead in some far-off land."

"No, no," said Eurycleia. "I can show thee that it is Odysseus indeed who is in the hall. On his foot is the scar that the tusk of a boar gave him in the old days. I spied it when I was washing his feet last night, and I would have told thee of it, but he clapped a hand across my mouth to stop my speech. Lo, I stake my life that it is Odysseus, and none other who is in the hall below."

Saying this she took Penelope by the hand and led her from the upper chamber into the hall. Odysseus was standing by a tall pillar. He waited there for his wife to come and speak to him. But Penelope stood still, and gazed long upon him, and made no step toward him.

Then said Telemachus, "Mother, can it be that thy heart is so hard? Here is my father, and thou wilt not go to him nor question him at all."

Said Penelope, "My mind is amazed and I have no strength to speak, nor to ask him aught, nor even to look on him face to face. If this is indeed Odysseus who hath come home, a place has to be prepared for him."

Then Odysseus spoke to Telemachus and said, "Go now to the bath, and make thyself clean of the stains of battle. I will stay and speak with thy lady mother."

"Strange lady," said he to Penelope, "is thy heart indeed so hard? No other woman in the world, I think, would stand so aloof from her husband who, after so much toil and so many trials, has come back after twenty years to his own hearth. Is there no place for me here, and must I again sleep in the stranger's bed?"

Said Penelope, "In no stranger's bed wilt thou lie, my lord. Come, Eurycleia. Set up for him his own bedstead outside his bed-chamber."

Then Odysseus said to her, speaking in anger: "How comes it that my bed can be moved to this place and that? Not a bed of that kind was the bed I built for myself. Knowest thou not how I built my bed? First, there grew up in the courtyard an olive tree. Round that olive tree I built a chamber, and I roofed it well and I set doors to it. Then I sheared off all the light wood on the growing olive tree, and I rough-hewed the trunk with the adze, and I made the tree into a bedpost. Beginning with this bedpost I wrought a bedstead, and when I finished it, I inlaid it with silver and ivory. Such was the bed I built for myself, and such a bed could not be moved to this place or that."

Then did Penelope know assuredly that the man who stood before her was indeed her husband, the steadfast Odysseus — none other knew of where the bed was placed, and how it had been built. Penelope fell a-weeping and she put her arms round his neck.

"O, Odysseus, my lord," she said, "be not angry with thy wife. Always the fear was in my heart that some guileful stranger should come here professing to be Odysseus, and that I should take him to me as my husband. How terrible such a thing would be! But now my heart is freed from all doubts. Be not angry with me, Odysseus, for not throwing myself on thy neck, as the women of the house did."

Then husband and wife wept together, and Penelope said, "It was the gods did this to us, Odysseus — the gods who grudged that we should have joy of the days of our youth."

Next they told each other of things that happened in the twenty years they were apart; Odysseus speaking of his own toils and sorrows, and Penelope telling what she had endured at the hands of the wooers. And as they told tales, one to the other, slumber came upon them, and the dawn found them sleeping side by side.

XVII

AND still many dangers had to be faced. The wooers whom Odysseus had slain were the richest and the most powerful of the lords of Ithaka and the Islands; all of them had fathers and brothers who would fain avenge them upon their slayer.

Now before anyone in the City knew that he had returned, Odysseus went forth to the farm that Laertes, his old father, stayed at. As he drew near he saw an old man working in the vineyard, digging round a plant. When he

came to him he saw that this old man was not a slave nor a servant, but Laertes, his own father.

When he saw him, wasted with age and all uncared for, Odysseus stood still, leaning his hand against a pear tree and sorrowing in his heart. Old Laertes kept his head down as he stood digging at the plant, and he did not see Odysseus until he stood before him and said:

"Old man, thou dost care for this garden well and all things here are flourishing — fig tree, and vine, and olive, and pear. But, if a stranger may say it, thine own self is not cared for well."

"Who art thou that dost speak to me like this?" old Laertes said, lifting his head.

"I am a stranger in Ithaka," said Odysseus. "I seek a man whom I once kindly treated — a man whose name was Odysseus. A stranger, he came to me, and he declared that he was of Ithaka, and that one day he would give me entertainment for the entertainment I had given him. I know not if this man be still alive."

Old Laertes wept before Odysseus. "Ah," said he, "if thou hadst been able to find him here, the gifts you gave him would not have been bestowed in vain. True hospitality thou wouldst have received from Odysseus, my son. But he has perished — far from his country's soil he has perished, the hapless man, and his mother wept not over him, nor his wife, nor me, his father."

So he spake and then with his hands he took up the dust of the ground, and he strewed it over his head in his sorrow. The heart of Odysseus was moved with grief. He sprang forward and fell on his father's neck and he kissed him, saying:

"Behold I am here, even I, my father. I, Odysseus, have come back to mine own country. Cease thy lamentation until I tell thee of the things that have happened. I have slain the wooers in mine hall, and I have avenged all their injuries and all their wrongful doings. Dost thou not believe this, my father? Then look on what I will show thee. Behold on my foot the mark of the boar's tusk — there it is from the days of my youth."

Laertes looked down on the bare foot, and he saw the scar, but still his mind was clouded by doubt. But then Odysseus took him through the garden, and he told him of the fruit trees that Laertes had set for him when he, Odysseus, was a little child, following his father about the garden — thirteen pear trees, and ten apple trees, and forty fig trees.

When Odysseus showed him these Laertes knew that it was his son indeed who stood before him — his son come back after twenty years' wandering. He cast his arms around his neck, and Odysseus caught him fainting to his breast, and led him into the house.

Within the house were Telemachus, and Eumæus the swineherd and Philœtius the cattleherd. They all clasped the hand of Laertes and their words raised his spirits. Then he was bathed, and, when he came from the bath, rubbed with olive oil he looked hale and strong. Odysseus said to him, "Father, surely one of the gods has made thee goodlier and greater than thou wert a while ago."

Said the old hero Laertes: "Ah, my son, would that I had such might as when, long before thou wert born, I took the Castle of Nericus there upon the Foreland. Would that in such might, and with such mail upon my shoulders, I stood with thee yesterday when thou didst fight with the wooers."

While they were speaking in this way the rumor of the slaying of the wooers went through the City. Then those who were related to the men slain went into the courtyard of Odysseus' house, and brought forth the bodies. Those who belonged to Ithaka they buried, and those who belonged to the Islands they put upon ships, and sent them with fisherfolk, each to his own home. Many were wroth with Odysseus for the slaying of a friend. He who was the most wroth was Eupeithes, the father of Antinous.

There was an assembly of the men of the country, and Eupeithes spake in it, and all who were there pitied him. He told how Odysseus had led away the best of the men of Ithaka, and how he had lost them in his ships. And he told them how, when he returned, he slew the noblest of the men of Ithaka and the Islands in his own hall. He called upon them to slay Odysseus, saying, "If we avenge not ourselves on the slayer of our kin we will be scorned for all time as weak and cowardly men. As for me, life will be no more sweet to me. I would rather die straightway and be with the departed. Up now, and let us attack Odysseus and his followers before they take ship and escape across the sea."

Many in that assembly put on their armor and went out

with old Eupeithes. And as they went through the town they met with Odysseus and his following as they were coming from the house of Laertes.

Now as the two bands came close to each other — Odysseus with Telemachus and Laertes; with the swineherd and the cattleherd; with Dolius, Laertes' servant, and with the six sons of Dolius — and Eupeithes with his friends — a great figure came between. It was the figure of a tall, fair and splendid woman. Odysseus knew her for the goddess Pallas Athene.

"Hold your hands from fierce fighting, ye men of Ithaka," the goddess called out in a terrible voice. "Hold your hands." Straightway the arms fell from each man's hands. Then the goddess called them together, and she made them enter into a covenant that all bloodshed and wrong would be forgotten, and that Odysseus would be left to rule Ithaka as a King, in peace.

So ends the story of Odysseus who went with King Agamemnon to the wars of Troy; who made the plan of the Wooden Horse by which Priam's City was taken at last; who missed the way of his return, and came to the Land of the Lotus-eaters; who came to the Country of the dread Cyclôpes, to the Island of Æolus and to the house of Circe, the Enchantress; who heard the song of the Sirens, and came to the Rocks Wandering, and to the terrible Charybdis, and to Scylla, past whom no other man had won scatheless; who landed on the Island where the Cattle of the Sun grazed, and who stayed upon Ogygia, the home of the nymph Calypso; so ends the story of Odys-

seus, who would have been made deathless and ageless by
Calypso if he had not yearned always to come back to his
own hearth and his own land. And spite of all his troubles
and his toils he was fortunate, for he found a constant wife
and a dutiful son and a father still alive to weep over him.